FREUD'S UNFINISHED JOURNEY.
Conventional and critical perspectives in psychoanalytic theory

Louis Breger

ROUTLEDGE & KEGAN PAUL
London, Boston and Henley

First published in 1981
by Routledge & Kegan Paul Ltd
39 Store Street,
London WC1E 7DD,
9 Park Street,
Boston, Mass. 02108, USA, and
Broadway House,
Newtown Road,
Henley-on-Thames,
Oxon RG9 1BN
Printed in the United States of America
by Fairfield Graphics
The Arcata Book Group
Copyright © Louis Breger, 1981

British Library Cataloguing in Publication Data

Breger, Louis
Freud's unfinished journey.
1. Freud, Sigmund
I. Title
150'.19'52   BF173.F85   80-41731
ISBN 0-7100-0613-6

CONTENTS

ACKNOWLEDGMENTS

I wish to express my appreciation to those colleagues and friends who generously gave their time and help as this book was being written. W. T. Jones has that all too rare ability to see things from another's point of view; his critical reading of the manuscript and many suggestions were most helpful. From the beginning, discussions with Robert Rosenstone shaped the book's course, as did his critical readings at more than one stage. Joseph M. Natterson's imprint is on the book in several important ways; I take this opportunity to thank him again. Other colleagues who offered useful critical readings of all or part of the manuscript include Victoria Hamilton and Herbert Morris.

Acknowledgment is made to the following for permission to reprint previously published material:

Sigmund Freud Copyrights Ltd, The Institute of Psycho-analysis and the Hogarth Press for permission to quote from the 'Standard Edition of the Complete Psychological Works of Sigmund Freud,' translated and edited by James Strachey.

W. W. Norton and Company, Inc. for permission to quote from 'An Autobiographical Study'and the'New Introductory Lectures on Psychoanalysis.'

Basic Books, Inc. for permission to quote from 'Studies on Hysteria,''the Interpretation of Dreams'and'Three Essays on the Theory of Sexuality.'

John Wiley & Sons, Inc. for permission to use a modified version of my article -Daniel Paul Schreber: From Male Into Female-, which first appeared in the 'Journal of the American Academy of Psychoanalysis' (1978), 6, 123-56.

1 ON READING FREUD

There are many ways to read Freud, perhaps as many as there are
readers. While profoundly influential, his work has inspired the
widest range of response: from loyal followers, to minor revision-
ists, to radical deviationists, to outright enemies. Those who work
directly with psychoanalytic theory have done so from a variety of
positions, ranging from the scientific-reductionistic to the
existential-humanistic. The scientifically inclined strive to 'objectify'
Freud's ideas while, at the other extreme, are those who would
dispense with theory entirely in favor of some sort of living-
feeling in the immediate moment. And then there are the orthodox –
the conservators – who attempt to preserve all that Freud said in
one vast, many-flavored, talmudic stew. What is true of theory is
true of clinical practice as well. Psychoanalysis is the starting
point for all contemporary types of psychotherapy, which have
flowered forth in a great variety of forms.

Freud's work lends itself to these many different responses because of its richness and complexity. The range of his interest
was so wide, his imagination so fertile, and his style of writing so
many-faceted that one often develops a new line of thought only
to discover that he anticipated it, or said the same thing in slightly
different words. One can find support for a great number of positions - even contradictory positions - somewhere in Freud's writings.

All of this is to say that one cannot simply read Freud and discover what he is saying - or undertake psychoanalytic training
and learn what he 'really' meant or acquire the single valid version
of psychoanalysis. One reads him from a particular perspective,
and this perspective has much to do with what one takes from the
reading. The reading is a work of interpretation and, like any
interpretation, it arises from the framework of the interpreter.
But it is precisely here, when one attempts to specify the framework within which to comprehend psychoanalysis, that difficulties
arise. Is psychoanalysis a science, to be understood, tested and
validated in accord with the rules and procedures of physics,
chemistry, biology, geology or astronomy? Or is it an art form
with its own esthetic truths to which the canons of science are
inapplicable? Should we move toward the validation of psychoanalytic hypotheses by controlled observation and experiment, or
can these truths be known only in the clinical context - in the
ongoing process of psychoanalytic therapy - from which they
arose? Or perhaps psychoanalysis is neither science nor art, but
simply an applied medical-psychological specialty, its essence the

healing of personal suffering. Or, in a very different way, perhaps it is a philosophy of life, a system of moral and ethical ideas
and values that guide our understanding of the great existential
issues. Or perhaps it is all of these? Or none of them.

Let us be sure that the issue under discussion is clear. In some
ways, all of the above are true of psychoanalysis: it has some of
the qualities of a science, it is an applied art with its own form
and procedures, it is a medical-psychological specialty, it is a
system of values and has many of the characteristics of a philosophy of life. In all these ways it both shares features with other
disciplines as well as presenting its own unique features. But
when we attempt to assess psychoanalysis – to determine the
validity of its propositions, hypotheses and theories, or decide
between alternative explanations – we become aware of the inadequacy or inappropriateness of traditional approaches. It is my
belief that, beyond the features it may share with science, with
applied or healing arts, or with western philosophical value
systems, psychoanalysis constitutes a unique endeavor that cannot be fully comprehended within the terms of these familiar disciplines. Further, I believe the failure to apprehend and explicitly
formulate the unique nature of psychoanalysis has led to numerous
unresolved arguments and disagreements, conflicts that very much
persist in contemporary uses of psychoanalytic theory. I hope, in
what follows, to clarify these conflicts by examining the assumptions and methods that make this approach to the human condition
unique.

The core of the problem is the mixture of old and new values
and models underlying Freud's work. Let us begin by looking at
the cultural and historical context in which Freud lived, the
starting place for psychoanalytic theory. Since a great deal has
been written about this I need only touch on the main features in
the briefest manner. Freud was educated in the liberal-rationalist
tradition and, while a cultural Jew, he proclaimed his atheism:
throughout his life his intellectual allegiance was to science and
reason. Indeed, his medical and research education imbued him
with a commitment to physicalist science, that materialist system
of values and priorities that persists to the present, not only in
many fields of psychology and social science but also, within
psychoanalysis, in those drawn to neurophysiological and other
mechanistic translations of theory. We know, too, that Freud was
a product of nineteenth-century European society, a society that,
despite many democratic reforms, remained male supremist. Freud's
views on men and women – on the essence of masculinity-femininity –
grew from this patriarchal Victorian soil and, while they moved
some distance from it, were never completely uprooted. Along with
the influence of these male-centered values, Freud was inevitably
influenced by other assumptions of his culture, chief among them
a belief in the necessity of hard work and the renunciation of
pleasure. That he was, in many ways, a most conventional bourg-
eois citizen, can be clearly seen in his personal life: his sexual
control and inhibitions, the long and distant courtship of his wife,

the conventional life style, his professional ambition and concern
for a prestigious position, his long and regular working hours,
even his patriotic fervor at the outset of the First World War.

In these ways he was very much a man – and I stress *man* –
of his times, as seen in his childhood identification with the
explorer-general Hannibal and his later view of himself as a 'con-
quistador.' And he could be very much the 'Herr Doktor Profesor',
concerned with the priorities of his discoveries, his image and his
status. Yet his creation – psychoanalysis – is a most revolutionary
challenge to all these beliefs and values. It poses the unconscious
as a powerful rival to reason and opens up the realm of the infantile, emotional and feminine that lies behind adult masculine
veneers. From the beginning, psychoanalytic work contains an
implicit challenge to conventional values and, in the late essays,
this trend is developed into a powerful critique of modern society.
This brings me to the key point: *Freud is a transitional figure
between the traditional values of nineteenth- and early twentieth-
century western society, and a radically new set of values – a
very different perspective, world view, guiding image or framework – which he creates in psychoanalysis, both as theory and
method*. We may contrast the old and new perspectives – the conventional nineteenth-century western world view with the new
psychoanalytic one – in three spheres. First, where the conventional position values science, objectivity and the life of reason,
the psychoanalytic view stresses the power of the unconscious,
of instinct, intuition, the emotional and subjective. It does not
glorify or worship these qualities but alerts us to their importance
and the necessity of coming to terms with them, of striking a
balance between reason and feeling, the objective and subjective.
Second, where the conventional position is male-centered, psychoanalysis brings psychological bisexuality to our awareness, it
shows how each outward form of exaggerated sexual identity has
its opposite, unconscious side. Related to this, psychoanalytic
exploration eventually leads to a deeper valuing of 'feminine-
maternal' qualities – feeling, intuition, love, caring, softness –
long deprecated by the male-dominated state. And, finally, where
the conventional view is just that: conventional – where it promotes
conformity to the mores of established society and adherence to
a work ethic that dictates the renunciation of pleasure and a
future-time orientation, Freud eventually proposes a profoundly
critical view of these values. In the final chapters of 'Civilization
and its Discontents', (1930) he points to just this work ethic –
in the form of the harsh and punitive superego – as a principal
source of the unhappiness and neurotic suffering of civilized man.
For purposes of discussion we may abbreviate these three areas
of transition in world view as: *from science to psychoanalysis*,
from male-centered to bisexual, and *from conventional to critical*.

I have said that Freud is a transitional figure between these
two world views and noted how his conventional personal life
contrasts with the revolutionary character of psychoanalysis as
method and theory. But it was not just his life style that conflicted

with the radical nature of the new theory and method he developed, for that would be of no more than minor biographical significance. The conflict – the unresolved ambivalence, if I may apply one of his own concepts to him – runs throughout much of psychoanalytic theory. That is to say, while Freud is a transitional figure between conventional views and the new insights that he, more than anyone else, enables us to see, the transition is never fully realized in his own work. There is a continual mixing of old and new assumptions, of progress to a fresh viewpoint and regression to the old, of radically new modes of understanding stated in a cumbersome language of the past. Hence, the unfinished journey.

Freud began his professional career in neurological research and, in 'The Project for a Scientific Psychology' (1895), attempted to formulate his developing theoretical ideas as a neurological model of the mind. In this model he tried to explain the *psychological* phenomena that concerned him – consciousness and the unconscious, pleasure and pain, imagination and rational thought – by positing physical-neurological processes as the underlying 'basis.' His commitment to this reductive approach was consistent with his medical-scientific training and, especially, the influences absorbed in Brücke's neurology laboratory. But, even at this early stage of his work, Freud recognized the inadequacy of this approach and he never published 'The Project.' In his next major work, 'The Interpretation of Dreams' of 1900, he moves entirely onto 'psychological ground.' As he states in the opening lines of that great work, its purpose is to

bring forward proof that there is a psychological technique which makes it possible to interpret dreams, and that, if that procedure is employed, every dream reveals itself as a psychical structure which has a meaning and which can be inserted at an assignable point in the mental activities of waking life (p. 1).

Dreams, associations and related aspects of the dreamer's life history are placed within the framework of a psychological theory, one that deals with meaning, interpretation, and symbolism. Dreams are decoded in terms of their symbolic meaning in relation to current and distant aspects of the dreamer's life, and in relation to major motivational conflicts. Nowhere in 'The Interpretation of Dreams,' nor in all of Freud's work that followed, was anything remotely neurological or physiological observed, nor was there ever any attempt to coordinate the theory with ongoing research in neurophysiology. In both his work with patients and the theory he developed, Freud had left the neurological laboratory and entered the world of psychoanalysis.

Yet, when he came to formulate a *general theory* a curious regression took place. In the final chapter of 'The Interpretation of Dreams,' the neuropsychological model of the mind developed in the earlier 'Project,' along with most of its reductive and mechanistic assumptions, finds its way back onto the purported psychological ground of the new approach. Chapter 7 contains the first major statement of what comes to be known as psychoanalytic 'metapsychology': a general theory whose concepts include psychic or libidinal energy, pleasure as energy discharge and pain as the accumulation of energy, the investment of this energy in 'objects' (cathexis), barriers to energy discharge, and related notions. In the metapsychology, the assumptions – and even many of the specific 'mechanisms' and terms – originally formulated in the neurological model of 'The Project,' were surreptitiously brought back into the new psychological theory.[1] As James Strachey puts it: ' "The Project," or rather its invisible ghost, haunts the whole series of Freud's theoretical writings to the very end' (1966, p. 290).

The persistence of the neurological model – with all its reductive trappings, its language of energies, discharge, mechanisms and objects – in the 'new' metapsychology is a major example of the way in which conventional concepts and values were mixed in with Freud's developing work. The metapsychology has remained a powerful influence, both as a theory itself and by the spread of its language into other key areas. In addition, the problems created by the mixture of old and new perspectives is not confined to the metapsychology or to areas directly infused with it. One encounters versions of this same problem in many other spheres: the theory of sexuality, hypotheses concerning the cause of neurosis, the model of anxiety, and conceptions of aggression and death. In each of these areas, new psychoanalytic insights are confounded with conventional values and assumptions, creating theoretical ambiguity and confusion that continues to the present.

Freud's first ideas concerning the role of sexuality in neurosis were clearly influenced by the sexual prejudices of his day. According to those conventional views, sexual pleasure was a dangerous force which had to be carefully controlled. Masturbation was seen as the cause of all sorts of weakness and illness – both physical and moral – and 'good' women were supposed to lack sexual interest or, indeed, passion of any sort. The picture of Victorian sexual life is well known. Freud's earliest theories of the role of sexuality in the creation of neurotic symptoms arose from these ideas; he believed that excessive masturbation led to a kind of psychic weakness while not enough of the right kind of sexual discharge could be equally pathological. He even invented a diagnostic category – 'actual neurosis' – in which dammed-up sex in the literal physical sense was supposed to result in neurotic symptoms. In these early theories anxiety, which was frequently observed in the neurotic patients, was thought to be a secondary result of misdirected sex, a sort of overflow of improperly channeled sexual energy.

The theories of sexuality, anxiety and neurosis all underwent a series of major transformations from these conventional origins. Freud discovered the importance of traumatic sexual experiences in childhood, then later came to believe these did not occur but were creations of the child's sexual wishes and fantasies. From the early ideas concerning the 'appropriate' discharge of sexual energy, came the central psychoanalytic theory of repression and defense, a theory which focuses on *inner conflict* between sexual wishes and moral strictures. The theory of anxiety also underwent a major transformation. From the early view in which anxiety was seen as a by-product of sexual discharge, there eventually developed a very different theory, one in which anxiety was viewed as the prior condition, 'signal', and motive for neurotic symptoms, inhibitions and defenses.

Freud's ideas became a major challenge to the oppressive sexual hypocrisy of the Victorian age, psychoanalysis a major source of liberation from excessive guilt, crippling inhibitions, and conventional prejudice. If we do not, today, view masturbation and infantile sexuality with horror, if we are more open-minded about a range of adult erotic activities – both hetero and homo sexual – and if we have abandoned the Victorian ideal of the passionless female, we have Freud, and the many who followed in his path, to thank.

Yet, paradoxically, Freud's own theories of sexuality, neurosis and anxiety – as well as his conceptions of masculinity-femininity, bisexuality and women – were never completely liberated from their conventional origins. The 'invisible ghost' of nineteenth-century sexual prejudice continues to haunt these theories, just as the ghost of 'The Project' haunts the metaphsychology. Sexuality – usually disguised in an abstract language of 'libidinal energy', 'id', and 'instinct' – is viewed as a disruptive force within the person. Women are seen as morally inferior, and 'passive-feminine' sexuality as a particularly dangerous inner temptation. In these ways, the conventional picture of sexuality was carried forth in the new theory in disguised form.

Similar ambiguities and confusions – again due to the incomplete transition in perspectives – may be found in other areas. The relative significance of sexual traumas and sexual wishes in the causation of neurosis never receives satisfactory theoretical treatment. And, while anxiety is given a more central position in the later essay devoted to it, this conception does not fully penetrate the larger theoretical structure. Similar difficulties cloud the theories of bisexuality and aggression and can be found in the conceptions of separation, loss and death. In each case, there is a paradoxical mixture of conventional male-centered assumptions and radical new psychoanalytic insights. In all these areas, the transition from the conventional to the new, critical, psychoanalytic perspective remains unfinished. I will present a detailed analysis of each of these areas in subsequent chapters.

Everyone who today deals with the phenomena from which Freud fashioned psychoanalytic theory – that is, all who explore the world of the unconscious, either in themselves or others; who work at psychoanalytic therapy, or one of its many variants; who encounter the pain, anxiety, guilt, depression and 'symptoms' of psychological disturbance in its many forms – are confronted with the same difficulties and dilemmas that he faced. For while our society has changed in many ways since Victorian days, reason, objectivity and science remain powerful ideals, as do the dictates of

work and conventionality. And, while there is much ferment
around male supremacy and women's rights, it remains to be
seen whether this will result in a shift of values from those
traditionally associated with masculinity, aggression and competition to those bound up with femininity, love and maternal care.
The dominant value structure of our society has not changed much
since Freud's time, the life of reason, work, clearly defined sex
roles and conventionality hold sway over any serious valuing of
ecstatic experience, bisexuality, or a truly critical examination
of our culture. The problems he faced in formulating a new psychoanalytic world view remain our problems still. In so far as we
understand these issues within Freud's work, we will be better
able to understand their current versions in our own work and
lives.
   In the chapters that follow, the consideration of Freud's unfinished journey will take us across a wide range of topics. I
will begin with a general discussion of the role of perspectives
or world views and then explore the essential features of the
dominant world view of the modern state. This will lead to a
consideration of the ideals of science and objectivity and their
place in that world view. An attempt will then be made to distinguish psychoanalysis from science, and to specify its unique
features. In part, the psychoanalytic approach can be characterized by its lack of commitment to any particular perspective; it
strives to understand perspectives - both personal and social -
from an outside position. To do this, one must set aside, at least
temporarily, conventional values and assumptions. One strives
toward the recognition of multiple truths and the critical-
comparative evaluation of different ways of life.
   Freud began his work in the male-centered world of nineteenth-
century Europe, a world that thought of man at war with nature
and in conflict with the instinctual core of his own nature. This
was a world view that valued men over women, 'masculine' qualities
over the 'feminine', work over the erotic, and science, reason and
objectivity over intuition, emotion and subjective experience. We
will see how he begins with a commitment to these assumptions and
develops a method that takes him to a very different position, one
associated with both sides of these dichotomies. He plunges into
the unconscious, the world of dreams, self-analysis, transference
and countertransference, neurotic suffering and insanity. And
in this realm, he discovers the psychological underworld of
respectable society, he comes face-to-face with the cost in personal
pain - anxiety, guilt, self-hatred and neurotic misery - that
results from his society's dominant way of life. His journey, begun
to understand neurosis and relieve the suffering of his patients,
took him to a much more revolutionary set of insights than he
was prepared for. He was then in conflict with the very substance
of his own way of life, as anyone is who makes revolutionary discoveries.
   The ambiguities of psychoanalytic theory result primarily from
this conflict between old and new perspectives. In his writings,

Freud is continually moving forward in radical directions and retreating to safe conventional ground, first revealing material that raises the most critical questions about his society's values and practices and then slipping back to side with those very values against society's victims. This unresolved conflict is played out in all the major areas of Freud's work: it is not confined to the metapsychology – though one finds it there in a striking way – but runs through the case studies, the theories of sexuality, neurosis and anxiety, and the conceptions of masculinity-femininity, bisexuality, aggression, loss, separation and death. I will discuss all of these areas in the chapters that follow, concluding with a close analysis of 'Civilization and its Discontents,' the work in which Freud comes closest to resolving these conflicts.

CODA

During a recent session with a patient in psychoanalysis I had an experience that I am sure occurs to all therapists from time to time. As I sat listening, I became aware of feeling completely lost amidst the maze of symptoms, dreams, associations and transference reactions: do I really understand any of this, I thought? This was a patient I knew well, a patient that I usually understood in a relatively clear way. Yet in this session, all that understanding seemed arbitrary, all past interpretations questionable. It then struck me, as I am sure it has many psychoanalysts before, what an amazing achievement Freud's creation of psychoanalysis was. How did he ever understand all this – the unconscious, the complications of neurosis and character, the subtle intricacies of transference – the first time around? Here I was, feeling at a loss to understand a patient, yet I had the benefit of all of Freud's discoveries, as well as the contributions of the very many others who have elaborated and built on the structure he created. He had none of this, no teachers, no supervisors, no reliable theoretical guidelines – indeed he had to ignore the misleading ideas and practices of the psychiatry of his time – as he invented, modified and elaborated psychoanalysis. He was a true genius; mankind is fortunate if one like him appears once in a century.

I do not mention Freud's genius here simply as a bit of hero-worship, but to clarify the stance toward him and his theories that will be taken in the present work. I believe his ideas are best approached with a critical spirit, yet I fear that some will feel this implies that Freud should have done things differently, that he is to be blamed for the ambiguities and conflicts – for the mixture of old and new world views – that characterize so much of psychoanalytic theory. This misses the point. Freud's contribution to our understanding of ourselves is much greater than anyone could possibly ask for. But it would be a betrayal of his own approach if we were to enshrine him as an infallible authority. The understanding of human psychology remains a difficult enterprise: we need as much clarity as we can achieve. Psychoanalytic theory contains such vital insights that it is worth extracting them from their often ambiguous surroundings. As we pursue this critical approach, we can be guided by Freud's own example: for he taught us to question, to look beneath surface appearances, to tease out underlying meaning, to continually modify theory in response to new observations, and to never accept the authority of a person or a theory because it occupies a *position* of authority, and that must include the authority of Freud's own genius.

2 PERSPECTIVES OLD
AND NEW

In 'The Forest People' the anthropologist Colin Turnbull presents
a sensitive account of life among the Mbuti Pygmies, one of the
few remaining hunting and gathering cultures left in the world.
The Pygmies live in a dense forest where immense trees and heavy
brush envelop them. Toward the end of his stay, Turnbull takes
Kenge, the young Mbuti who has served as his friend and guide,
for a tour of the world outside the forest – a world the Pygmies
barely know. They drive over a ridge and come upon a vast open
plain where many animals can be seen, including a large herd of
buffalo grazing a few miles away. 'What insects are those?' asks
Kenge, pointing to the buffalo. Turnbull realizes that Kenge has
lived his entire life in surroundings where trees limit his range
of vision so that he has never learned to use the cues that we
rely on when making judgments of size over distance for, after
all, the distant buffalo do look tiny. He attempts to explain that
they are large buffalo, but far away, only to be laughed at and
called a liar by his Pygmy friend. As they drive down among the
animals, Kenge becomes frightened, and Turnbull 'was never
able to discover just what he thought was happening – whether he
thought the insects were changing into buffalo, or that they were
miniature buffalo growing rapidly as we approached. His only
comment was that they were not real buffalo and he was not going
to get out of the car again until we left the park' [1961, p. 253].
   This interesting vignette shows how an aspect of our perception
of the world that we learned at an early age and perform auto-
matically – making compensations for the size of objects in terms
of their distance from us – is not automatic for a perceiver with
different prior experiences. It shows that what anyone auto-
matically and naturally sees as *real*, and regards as independent
of himself, is neither automatic nor natural but a function of
his perceptual *set*, his framework or paradigm. One might argue
that Turnbull's view of the buffalo was the 'real' one – was more
valid, true, scientific or whatever – but that would be equating
the real with the perceptual framework of a particular culture.
As he found when he lived in the Pygmies's forest world, many
of the sets, frameworks and assumptions that he brought with
him as a western anthropologist interefered with his ability to
function in the well-adapted way they did with their cultural sets.
Within the forest, the Pgymy perception of reality worked very
well indeed while, obviously, Turnbull's is better suited to life
among television, automobiles and supermarkets. The example
also calls attention to the fear that can be aroused when an

established set is challenged; it is indeed frightening when the 'reality' that one knows so well begins to change or act in unexpected or unpredictable ways.

This small example is meant to illustrate a much larger point: our perception of reality is a transaction between something 'out there' and something 'inside' - the something inside being variously labeled *set*, *framework*, *schema*, *perspective*, *paradigm*, *guiding image* or *world view*.[1] The psychology of perception contains numerous demonstrations of the role of such sets. So does the large-scale study of the development of cognition or intelligence, carried out by Jean Piaget and his many followers. Piaget's work is both based on, and provides much evidence for, a *transactional* approach to reality. It shows how one must take into account the changing schemes that affect the apprehension of reality, how the child lives in a shifting series of different cognitive-perceptual 'worlds' as his schemas undergo successive stages of development. For the infant the world consists of sensations and actions; it ceases to exist when he does not see, hear, feel, taste or act on it. The young child apprehends the world through intuitive, fantasy-laden schemas: he cannot clearly distinguish his idiosyncratic imaginative view from the shared or consensual view of others. And, for the adolescent and adult, a more abstract, reasoned, socialized mode of thought is possible. At each major stage of development the child lives in a somewhat different 'reality' because the schemas he has available for transaction with the world are different.

A related position is outlined by the linguist-anthropologist Benjamin Whorf [1956] with respect to language. Any particular language contains tendencies - certain predispositions to see, think, categorize and define - which influence the speaker/listener's apprehension of reality. Like the sets of perception and the schemas of intellect, the structure of language plays its role in our transaction with the world.

CULTURAL PERSPECTIVES

These examples of the constructive role of set, schema and language structure in the apprehension of reality open up an approach that we may now explore in a more general way. Any culture, subculture, society or historical period can be characterized in terms of its sets, perspectives or world views - the guiding assumptions, beliefs, values and categories that determine the way 'reality' is constructed. The members of a society have their own version of its world view, a version that is shared with others in the group, while also containing idiosyncratic features that result from the person's unique life experience. In what follows, I wish to explore this general model of social and personal perspectives and then apply it to Freud, his society and the development of psychoanalytic theory.

Thomas Kuhn's [1962] analysis of the role of paradigms in the development of physical science is well known and will serve as a starting point. Kuhn contrasts his historical study of science with that found in the typical science textbook. Textbooks are written as if there is a reality 'out there' that scientists discover more and more about as their techniques and theories progressively advance. Kuhn calls this the 'accretion' view and, as we can see, it rests on an assumption very different from the transactional or constructivist position just examined. The traditional position – and many scientists still share this view – tends to neglect the role of the belief structure of the scientist-observer or, what is the same thing, assumes that the particular way reality is perceived is how the world 'really' is. Kuhn argues that the historical study of progress in a variety of scientific fields does not support this textbook account. Rather, he finds that scientists are powerfully influenced by their belief structures, the paradigms which are acceptable at the time they are working. Each paradigm defines what is worth observing (and therefore leaves out much else), specifies the correct methods and acceptable procedures for gathering data (and assumes other methods to be worthless), and dictates what is known and what questions remain to be answered. In short, the scientist works in a world which is narrowly hemmed-in by his paradigm and this narrowness is useful for the progress of what Kuhn calls 'normal science' – progress within an established field such as physical mechanics after Newton, chemistry after Lavoisier, or electromagnetics after Maxwell.

Large advances in science – what Kuhn calls 'scientific revolutions' – usually do not arise within the relatively closed world of an accepted paradigm, but, rather, come about when great innovations – created by a Newton, Einstein or Darwin – force a shift to a different paradigm. Once a shift is made, what were before peripheral or unimportant observations can take on new significance, while old puzzles and questions are resolved or become less interesting. Whole new areas, along with new methods, are often opened up. Examples would be physics after Newton or, after the invention of Quantum Mechanics, biology after Darwin, or genetics after Mendel. The great leaps in science are often matters of paradigm shift rather than the gradual accretion of knowledge within an existing framework.

Kuhn's analysis is one of several that demonstrate the role of paradigms in science. During the 'normal science' phase, when research proceeds within accepted boundaries, the paradigm itself is more or less invisible. It operates like the automatic sets of perception or the structure of a language that is taken for granted by the fluent speaker. Scientific revolutions, because they involve a shift in paradigm, can create an awareness of these typically invisible assumptions and values. This is important, for many who are taken with science are unaware that even such seemingly objective fields as physics, chemistry or biology do, in fact, involve subjective factors: the scientist's paradigms. Indeed, there is a tradition in the West that gives special status to the 'reality' defined by science, that sees it as equivalent with the 'real' or 'objective' world. Yet, even here, we see how 'reality' is a construction, how it is only known through the subjective belief structure – the paradigm – of the observer.

Kuhn's account of paradigms and paradigm shifts is confined to physical science. If we step back from the fields he surveys, we see that science itself – even with its many shifts and revolutions – constitutes a larger paradigm or world view. It consists of a particular way of approaching, 'seeing' and working with reality that contrasts with other, quite different, approaches. A perceptive account of these larger paradigms is provided by my friend and colleague, the philosopher W. T. Jones (1972), who calls them 'world views.' As he puts it:

> For me a paradigm is simply the world view that happens to be dominant in any society at any particular time. It includes the way of doing science at a particular time and also the particular set of beliefs about the world that are held to be 'true' at the time, but it includes more than that – it is the whole perspective, learned at mother's knee and then refined and corrected at school and college, from which one looks at the world. It is a complex lens through which we view the world. This perspective is so pervasive that most of us, most of the time, see through the lens without noticing it. That is, most of us are, metaphysically speaking, naive realists: we assume that the world we see through the lens of our particular paradigm is 'out there' just as we happen to see it. To loosen a paradigm is precisely to become aware of the lens, to become aware of the fact that the world we are seeing is merely the world as seen from a particular perspective (Jones, 1977, p. 5).

Two central world views are those that Jones calls 'Naturwissenschaft' and 'Geisteswissenschaft.' The first is associated with the values and practices of the natural sciences; within its framework the world is viewed in terms of discrete entities – whether atoms, cells, chemical elements, or behaviors – which are to be isolated and manipulated, as 'variables' in experiments, for instance. The goal of such work is the discovery of general or abstract explanatory and predictive theories. The other paradigm – associated, for instance, with the Romantic movement of the last century, the Existential tradition in philosophy, literature and drama, or with certain forms of religion – tends to view the world in terms of dynamic, continuous processes which cannot be meaningfully isolated from their context. The emphasis here is on the individual, on immediate and concrete experience, as contrasted with the abstractions of the first paradigm. Jones argues that the 'Naturwissenschaft' view has long been dominant in the West with the 'Geisteswissenschaft' a contrapuntal minority voice. As one can see, these two broad world views overlap with the two psychoanalytic frameworks that I began to outline in the last chapter. In these terms, Freud begins with the world view of science – of 'Naturwissenschaft' – and moves toward an appreciation of the submerged values of 'Geisteswissenschaft.'

Psychoanalysis is not to be equated with this second perspective, however, but with the attempt to explore and understand all perspectives from a position of 'neutrality' and openness to multiple points of view.

But this begins to sound terribly impersonal and psychoanalysis is, if anything, a very intimate, personal enterprise. How is this side of analytic work to be brought in? This question can be approached with the idea of personal perspectives - the aspect that Jones refers to as 'learned at mother's knee.' For a world view is not confined to one's work, profession or scientific theory; it pervades all sides of life. Like the perception of reality within a scientific paradigm, we tend to be naive realists with respect to our personal-cultural perspectives; that is, we unconsciously assume that the way we see and feel about core areas of human social experience are the way these areas 'really' are. In order to appreciate the role of our personal perspectives, we must, figuratively speaking, get outside of them. There are different ways to do this; one is by examining, in as open-minded a fashion as possible, the formation of world views in cultures or historical periods very different from our own.

As examples, I am going to describe two areas of childhood experience - the feeding of infants and the imposition of discipline - in two very different societies: the !Kung Bushmen of Southwest Africa and the seventeenth-century French. But first, let me say why I have chosen these areas and these societies. Few would disagree that the satisfaction of hunger comprises a core motivational system for all human beings. Whether one calls hunger an instinct, a drive, a primary motive or whatever, it is clearly one of the central energizing and organizing forces of human activity. Along with this motivational primacy we find great variability across cultures and persons in how they satisfy this basic need. The obtaining of food, its distribution and the way it is consumed are involved in all sorts of religious rituals, from the potlatches of the Northwest Coast Indians to Hebrew dietary laws. Having a lot to eat or very little, being obese or thin, eating with refined manners or with little concern for appearance - all illustrate how hunger, food and its consumption are interconnected with considerations of beauty, prestige, power, anxiety, morality and love. In short, the feelings of hunger, the activity of eating, and the results in physical appearance, are all perceived through value systems - through world views. The unthinkable food taboos of one culture are the sacred rites of another.

The very different food practices of different societies begin with the feeding of infants. And, from the individual's point of view, his first experience with hunger and its satisfaction gives an initial stamp to the personal-cultural perspective that will later have wide connections with his perception of the human world as nurturant or frustrating, loving or indifferent, trustworthy or unstable.

A similar analysis can be applied to the child's first experience

with discipline and the imposition of social rules. All cultures
train their children, but the range with respect to when it is
begun, who does it, and how it is carried out is enormous. There
are societies that believe infants must be disciplined in the first
months of life and those which don't seem to bother much for
several years. Practices range from the most severe to the most
lenient, and the areas selected as the targets of discipline –
toileting and cleanliness, 'manners,' sexuality, the expression
of anger and aggression, adherence to cultural taboos, rites
and rituals – vary most widely. Again, as with hunger and feeding, the child's first encounter with discipline gives an initial
form to a personal perspective that will encompass the perennial
conflicts between individual autonomy and social conformity. In
sum, an examination of feeding and discipline in different societies
should illuminate the range of variation in these core personal
areas.

But why the !Kung and seventeenth-century France? I have
selected these as examples from the myriad other societies and
historical periods because they are particularly clear examples
of two broad types of cultural organization. The !Kung are a
small hunting and gathering society whose mode of life closely
approximates the form of human social organization that was
characteristic of our species for many thousands – probably
hundreds of thousands – of years. While homo sapiens in its
modern form has been in existence for 60,000 years, students
of human evolution agree that the essential features of culture –
language, the use of tools, fire and social organization – go back
at least ten times that far. For most of this long period of time
members of the human species lived in small nomadic bands,
hunting wild animals and gathering wild vegetation. This hunter-
gatherer existence is the earliest form of human culture that we
know anything about. It is only within the past 10,000 years,
a short time by archeological standards, that men began to
domesticate plants and animals and, as recently as 2,000 years
ago – a time we associate with the Roman Empire and the beginning
of Christianity – one-half of the human population on earth still
lived in hunter-gatherer societies. The !Kung are one of the few
hunter-gatherer societies to survive relatively intact into modern
times. Excellent accounts of !Kung life have been given by
several sensitive anthropologists and my examples of feeding and
discipline will be drawn from these studies.[2] This is probably
as close as we will ever come to primitive man – to a picture of
life before the beginnings of civilization.

As a contrast to the !Kung I have chosen seventeenth-century
France to represent the immense range of civilized societies. These
spread from the African and Middle Eastern 'states' to ancient
Egypt, Greece and Rome, through the Middle Ages, to the con-
temporary societies of Europe and America. And this is just in
the West; one might trace related genealogies in China, Japan,
India and Latin America. I chose to focus on France of the 'Early
Modern' period, the seventeenth century, for several reasons.

One is the availability of fairly extensive and reliable information on feeding and discipline during this period.[3] But more important is what this society represents. France in the seventeenth century was emerging from the Middle Ages; it was one of the first of the modern European states. Many of the practices we will examine display, in crude and sometimes exaggerated form, the characteristics of these new, centralized and powerful nations. Over the next two centuries, these countries came to dominate the world; and the values of nineteenth-century Europe, the context of Freud's early work, began here. Thus, another reason for the choice of this particular society; the sets and predispositions inculcated in children in seventeenth-century France, which contrast so sharply with those among the !Kung, are crude early versions of the world view of Freud and the members of his culture.

The first encounter we have with our society occurs shortly after birth when, as infants, we are cared for by our mothers. Let us begin with a comparison of feeding and infant care in these two different societies. !Kung infants are in more or less continuous contact with their mothers' bodies from birth onwards. When separations begin, they are initiated by the infant when he is old enough to begin exploration, and not by the mother. Feeding is from the mother's breast on a complete and continuous demand basis. The infant nurses as much as he wants, whenever he wants: average time between onset of fretting and beginning of feeding is six seconds. Supplementary feeding and/or solid foods are not introduced until the second or third year and weaning from the breast does not occur until the next pregnancy, usually when the infant is three. Weaning from being carried by the mother occurs around age four when the next infant is born. The vigorous breast feeding, in combination with diet and other factors such as the mother's body weight, produce a contraceptive effect so that new pregnancies are delayed. This delay and the resulting long time span between infants allows the mother to devote a great deal of time and attention to each child for the first three to four years of its life.

This long period of nurturance and secure attachment exists within a society where such practices are viewed as completely natural - as demanded by human nature, we might say; it is supported by the adult members of the group who had experienced it in their own infancies, of course. From the infant's point of view, food from mother's breast is immediately forthcoming when he is hungry; there are very few frustrations, delays or inconsistencies. What is more, such experiences are not confined to nursing; physical contact with the mother and other members of the band is available in a similarly consistent and nonfrustrating way, and there is a good deal of open sensual play and stimulation. All of these early experiences give an initial direction to the child's world view; they foster what Bowlby terms 'secure attachment' or what Erikson calls a sense of 'basic trust' in relation to one's own body, to other persons, and to

the environment. One sees the spread of this trust and security
in the !Kung's feeling about the world. As adults they live and
feel themselves to be in a trusting ecological balance with their
fellows and the surrounding environment. They are on 'intimate'
terms with the animals they hunt and exhibit little anxiety over
food, even during periods of drought or poor hunting. They
have extensive personal knowledge about food resources - wild
animals and plants - and feel them there, ever present, for the
taking. These experiences with nursing, physical contact and
secure attachment play an important early part in the formation
of this wider world view. The !Kung, much more than the members of many Western societies, experience themselves as part
of nature, as connected to, rather than alienated from, the
world around them.

The feeding of infants in seventeenth-century France contrasts
sharply with the practices just described. France at this time
was a monarchy emerging from the feudalism of the Middle Ages.
It was a power-oriented culture that valued males and male
activities over the female, the rich over the poor, and those who
possessed important resources - land, title, social position - over
those who did not. The distribution of food in infancy was strongly
influenced by these class and power relations. Adequate diet,
secure nursing and a stable attachment during the earliest years
of life were very uncertain. The infant mortality rate ranged
from 25 to 75 per cent, and infanticide was practiced in both
overt and subtle forms. There seemed little faith that a mother
could simply nurse her own child: many practices and beliefs
interfered with the establishment of an adequate nursing bond.
A gruel, of dubious nutritional value and almost certainly con-
taminated with germs, was introduced early into the infant's
diet. The wealthier families gave their infants out to wet nurses -
often to peasant families in the country - and sometimes did not
see either child or nurse for several years. And poor mothers
were forced to share their milk with the infants of the rich. For
many mothers, a new pregnancy every year was the rule,
placing a heavy burden of child care on them. Nursing, and
maternal activities more generally, were depreciated as part of
the generally male-centered value system that infused the
society at large.

As in the case of the !Kung, we just think in terms of a cyclical or interactive process. The experience of the seventeenth-
century French infant induced frustration, high levels of anxiety
over food, love, maternal care, and the human environment more
generally. Those who survived infancy were well on their way to
becoming anxious, angry, insecure, grasping individuals who
feared for the sustenance necessary for survival - a character
structure, motivational set, or world view that well prepared
them for life in this French society.

Now, let us turn our attention to discipline and the imposition
of social control in these two cultures. Here is a typical example
from the !Kung, as reported by the anthropologist Patricia Draper:

One afternoon I watched for two hours while a father hammered and shaped the metal for several arrow points. During the period his son and his grandson (both under four years old) jostled him, sat on his legs, and attempted to pull the arrow heads from under the hammer. When the boys' fingers came close to the point of impact, he merely waited until the small hands were a little further away before he resumed hammering. Although the man remonstrated with the boys (about once every three minutes), he did not become cross or chase the boys off; and they did not heed his warnings to quit interfering. Eventually, perhaps fifty minutes later, the boys moved off a few steps to join some teenagers lying in the shade (Lee and DeVore, 1976, p. 206).

What a wealth of insight into father-child relations is captured in this scene! Would one of us ever act this way? We live in a world where adult 'work' - which is deemed important - is segregated from children's 'play' - which is assumed to be of little value. Children who interfere with a man's work are likely to be disciplined: 'Hands off,' 'Can't you see Daddy's working?' and so on. The !Kung father doesn't act this way because he operates from an entirely different value system concerning work, play and interconnection of the world of children and adults. He is not driven to work hard, either by others or himself - there is no 'work ethic,' no valuing of work as a good thing in itself - and he does not feel guilty when he is free, or playing or just sitting around. Hence he is accepting of the children's curiosity and does not resent their freedom; he does not feel the need to control, shape, train or discipline their curious, playful or 'unsocialized' impulses since he was not disciplined this way himself and does not have such an inner orientation toward his own impulses.

The permissive and nonpunitive approach of this !Kung father is typical of their more general approach to discipline. There is nothing at all like our cleanliness or toilet training: as they grow, children learn to defecate away from the camp by imitating older children. The curiosity and exploration that is so much a part of every child is encouraged and almost never punished, as the above example illustrates. Even the child's anger and aggression toward adults is handled in a way far different from what we know. For instance, the child who has a temper tantrum when his mother refuses to nurse or carry him is allowed to spend his rage in cries and blows which the mother fends off. The mother is not threatened, she does not consider the attack an affront to her dignity, and the child is not stopped immediately nor punished, either of which would induce further frustration. Since the !Kung do not value or encourage interpersonal fighting, children must eventually learn to channel their aggression elsewhere, for instance into hunting. But adults do not react to the child's rage at frustration as something 'bad' which must be trained or disciplined out of him.

The general effect of the !Kung's approach to discipline is to

create personal-social perspectives of a relatively guilt-free
nature. Their early experience with a permissive, nonpunitive
social world leads to a valuation of individuality over compliance,
to personal autonomy over conformity. Primitive societies do not
have leaders or chiefs and nothing like laws or tight social
restrictions.

As was the case with feeding, the area of discipline in
seventeenth-century France provides a sharp contrast with that
observed among the !Kung. Infants were routinely swaddled –
wrapped in tight bindings that prevented them from moving their
legs and arms. Thus, beginning in the first year, there was an
attempt to control the child's autonomy. Such attempts became
pronounced from the second year on – a period at which children
become more curious, and, of great importance, when they begin
to test their independence and 'will' against the adult world.
French parents at this time saw the child's newly emerging
autonomy as potentially dangerous 'willfulness' and 'disobedience'
and it was routinely the object of harsh disciplinary measures.
Indeed, the goal of such training was to make children obey
adults, and defiance – even minor or symbolic acts of the child –
became the excuse for blows, deprivations, whippings and other
forms of brutality. The Dauphin, later Louis XIII, whose childhood is extensively documented, was administered a daily whipping, whether he had misbehaved or not, as a way of 'breaking
his will.' His father, King Henry IV, who had himself been
subjected to such whippings as a child, simply felt he was doing
his parental duty by having his son whipped – doing what was
required to stamp out evil childish willfulness. Such practices
were widespread – they were not confined to France and continued
in Europe into the twentieth century – and they left their mark
on the developing child. The child, exposed to these disciplinary
practices, came to feel anxious and guilty about his autonomous-
independent strivings, as well as about his anger toward the
oppressive authorities.

To sum up: each society, the primitive !Kung and the
seventeenth-century French, feeds, cares for, disciplines and
trains their children in ways that both arise from the society's
world view – the way male and female, mother- and fatherhood,
love, hunger, nurturance, autonomy, obedience and disobedience
are conceived – *and* passes these defined views into the next
generation by creating the culturally appropriate predispositions
in the developing child. These experiences with feeding, physical
contact, love, permissiveness and discipline, begun in infancy
and repeated through childhood, form the individual's intuitive
basis for his feelings about his own nature, as manifested in the
most basic processes of body and human interaction. This core
personal perspective then becomes elaborated, within the context
of family and society, into a deeply ingrained set of predispositions, a world view concerned with human impulses, feelings and
actions. Clearly, if our prototypical !Kung and French infants
each grew up to be psychological theorists, they would formulate

very different theories on the basis of their deeply ingrained
personal-cultural experience.

PRIMITIVE AND CIVILIZED WORLD VIEWS

Let me now attempt a more general statement of the world views
inculcated by these two very different forms of social experience.
The primitive lives in a world of close and intimate contact with
other persons and the surrounding world of nature. His own
inner nature - hunger, the need for physical contact and attachment, sensual or curious actions, anger and aggression - meets
with generally accepting responses from the adults he encounters.
These experiences, repeated through the life cycle and supported
by others in the group, form the core of a world view which may
be called *human-within-nature*. This orientation extends both
outward and inward; that is, it colors his perception of both the
outside world, toward which the primitive feels a close attachment,
and his experience of his own impulses, emotions, fantasies and
actions, which are felt as potentially harmonious with social life.

The contrasting experience of Western man of the past few
centuries produces a very different world view, one which may be
called *man-against-nature*. Repeated experiences of frustration,
insufficient nourishment, disrupted attachment, constricted
autonomy and harsh discipline lead to the perception of the world
of other persons - and the environment more generally - as un-
trustworthy, dangerous, punitive, ungiving; in short, as enemies
with which one must struggle. A similar orientation towards one's
own nature results from the experience typical of the modern
world. That is, repeated frustrations, punishments and inconsistent gratification create feelings of anxiety and guilt about one's
own hunger, sensual-sexual urges, autonomous strivings and
anger at authority; these too come to be experienced as enemies
that one must combat in order to survive.

I am deliberately using the terms 'human' and 'man' in labeling
these two world views to capture another aspect of the values
involved. In the primitive mode of life, there is much greater
equality of the sexes and much less overevaluation of one sex,
or the qualities associated with it, at the expense of the other.
These societies are not androgynous: men know they are men and
women women, and there are many defined activities and social
groupings along sex lines. Yet they are less anxious and rigid
about sex-role distinctions; they are more accepting of 'feminine'
qualities in men and 'masculine' qualities in women. [4] Western
culture, on the other hand, has a long history in which special
valuation is given to men - to a male god, to fathers, to sons
over daughters - and to qualities associated with masculinity;
aggression, toughness, what can be termed the warrior-hero
ethos. Along with this male-centered value system, there has been
a rather rigid enforcement of sex-role segregation and a good
deal of anxiety over threatened sex-role blending. Thus, the

'man' in *man-against-nature* is meant to emphasize that the world view of the modern state contains these patricentric values; and it is typically the creation of men - of kings and rulers, of male philosophers and scientists.

These two broad world views - the *human-within-nature*, and the *man-against-nature* - are characteristic of these two broad forms of social-cultural organization. The first is found in primitive society: the hunter-gatherer form of cultural organization, seen in the long early period of our existence as a species. It has also been found, to one degree or another, in various societies, subcultures, families, individuals, religious movements and backwaters of the modern state. [5] The second world view is associated with Western culture and can be seen most strikingly in the states which consolidated themselves in Europe and America during the last four hundred years and which now, as modern industrialized nations, dominate the globe. This is the view which sees the human species as special, as set off from the natural world, as constructing its own environment as a protection against what is felt to be a hostile, grudging nature. Those living in accord with this view have always singled out some major sphere of human impulse - willfulness, sexual pleasure, curiosity, anger - and made it the object of disciplinary attacks.

The personal or experiential quality of these two broad orientations can be described in terms of *wholeness* versus *alienation*. The primitive feels himself to be a connected part of an integrated whole; he is attached to the other persons in his band, to the world of plants and animals, and to his own impulses, cravings and actions. Alienation, splitting, the suppression, repression or separation of man from the world - and from aspects of his own experience - are integral parts of the rise of the modern state. And just as the 'war against nature' is never 'won,' so the attempt to split off or repress aspects of one's own nature is never completed. Those parts of the person deemed enemies - sexuality and the 'feminine'; autonomous, willful and rebellious potentials; childlike, free and playful qualities - live on in the unconscious. They are felt as unwanted, foreign intruders, ever trying to gain entry into the civilized-socialized self.

At this point the reader may complain that I am slipping in a large and very speculative argument under the cover of a general discussion of the nature of perspectives or world views. And he would be right - for I have moved from that general discussion to a consideration of the idea of personal perspectives, to examples from one primitive and one modern society, and then taken a great leap to a discussion of the world views characteristic of primitive and civilized life, in the broadest terms. And I have indulged in some impossibly large generalizations. Not all primitives are exactly like the !Kung nor, clearly, is seventeenth-century France typical of the great range of Western societies of the past four hundred years. One could undoubtedly find many counterexamples and points of disagreement. Nevertheless, I will stand by my general thesis: there are clusters of values, child-rearing practices, orientations toward male and female, and toward sexuality, aggression and childhood - in short, world views - that are characteristic of these two broad cultural types. I argue, further, that these two world views are regularly accompanied by the two kinds of personal styles: the holistic, human-within-nature and the alienated, man-against-nature. And I believe a survey of the anthropological and historical evidence would give *general* support to this thesis, though obviously I cannot present that material here without writing a whole additional book. I ask the reader to provisionally accept the thesis from the small amount of evidence presented so far, in order to see how it bears up when applied to the topic that is our central concern: the transition in perspectives within psycho-analytic theory.

Having completed a general discussion of world views and the transactional or constructive approach to reality, and having sketched out the world view characteristic of the modern state, we are now ready to pick up the discussion begun earlier and examine the society and values where Freud's work began.

THE WORLD VIEW OF THE MODERN STATE

The intellectual climate of nineteenth-century Europe was dominated by the triumphs of physical science, by the conquest of 'backward' societies by the technologically superior European nations and by the glorification of man's intelligence - of reason - as a virtue or end unto itself. At the same time, the various scientific, philosophical and popular versions of this world view existed in societies which had many of the trappings of authori-tarian and militaristic rule. Freud's Vienna was the capital of an empire and, while democratic freedoms were certainly increasing in comparison to earlier periods, only a minority of the popula-tion benefited from them. Most of the European states were, as many have recently stressed, male supremist societies in which the roles and activities open to women were decidedly limited. Marked differences in wealth kept the poor in a similar position of inferiority and limited opportunity. And if children were not as harshly treated as they had been in seventeenth-century France, they were still subjected to a considerable amount of authoritarian and often quite punitive and frightening discipline. Sexuality, as Freud's own work was to show, was a hotbed of conflict, anxiety and guilt. The double standard of male-female sexual conduct was everywhere in evidence: women were expected to remain chaste and pure, or were cast into the world of prosti-tution. While men were allowed much greater sexual freedom, they suffered their own forms of guilt and conflict. The sensual pleasures of childhood had become the bête noire of reform-minded adults, who seemed gripped with a kind of 'masturbation insanity': they saw the autoerotic activities of children as the cause of illness, character faults and mental weakness of all kinds and directed severe disciplinary efforts at stamping them out.

In these and many other ways, these European societies outwardly valued men over women; work and discipline over the erotic and play; toughness and success over softness, love and freedom; in general, a set of qualities associated with male-aggression over maternal love - not surprising since they were in the line of two thousand years of patricentric Western civilization, buttressed by the Judeo-Christian tradition with its powerful male deity. This picture of nineteenth-century morality mainly characterizes the middle classes, of course. Aristocratic men and women were not bound by it, nor were many peasants and members of the lower classes. But, many recent historians have pointed out, it was precisely this middle class morality that more and more came to dominate European culture; so it is valid to see its dictates as the defining values of the period.

By the nineteenth century Western culture had, if anything, become more competitive, status-oriented and aggressive. Scientific and technological progress not only led directly to the manufacture of armaments, but was part of the 'conquest' of nature and the 'exploitation' of natural resources, described in fittingly warlike imagery. And the productivity of industrial nations required workers who were disciplined and reliable, who could serve as efficient cogs in the factory, the bureaucracy and the army. Compulsory schooling was the norm and, along with a cluster of related child-rearing techniques, helped inculcate the work ethic, the guilt and anxiety, self-discipline and post-ponement of the pleasures of the present for an ever-receding future, all required by life in an industrial society.

Civilization was not so one-dimensional as the above account makes it seem, of course. There were always countercurrents and countervoices. The nineteenth century saw the Romantic movement, which came to include major figures in the arts - poets, writers, painters, playwrights - which gave expression to a set of 'feminine' qualities quite at odds with the dominant values of the time. And the turn of the century saw further develop-ments in art, drama, literature and philosophy that broke with traditional forms to explore the world of feeling, subjectivity and the nonrational. And, of course, there were many democratic and socialist movements for reform - women's rights, child labor laws and related efforts to soften the treatment of children, attempts to humanize the factories and the institution of social welfare programs in the cities. Even when the dominant value system was in force, there were always individual exceptions: strong women who refused to accept a passive role, men who criticized and objected to authority and warfare, and families that attempted to raise their children with a greater balance of love and acceptance over harsh discipline. But these remained exceptions, countercurrents against a strong and clearly more powerful set of values. And it was this dominant world view - a

view that extolled science, reason, work and the masculine
virtues - that prevailed during Freud's formative years.
   Let us examine one specific illustration of these trends and
countertrends, one that directly impinged on Freud's own
developing ideas. The triumphs of science and technology gave
tremendous impetus to a cluster of values associated with a
physicalist-materialist approach to life, an approach that strongly
valued reason and objectivity. Many who were committed to these
values were firmly convinced that real progress in many fields
was equivalent to the spread of science. Thus, there were
attempts to extend the scientific approach from physics and
chemistry into biology, psychology and the study of society,
and even the traditional preserves of religion: ethics and moral
philosophy. This attempt to make the scientific ideal a defining
standard did not go unchallenged. It was countered by those who
argued that the approach of physical science was inappropriate
to the study of man and society. They spoke of an élan vital, a
vital or life force, that distinguished the living from the inorganic
and that demanded a different form of understanding. This
challenge to the spread of rationalist-materialist values drew on
vitalistic and nature philosophies associated with the Romantic
movement. Those concerned with extending the scope of science
saw these vitalistic and Romantic values as a regressive pull
toward the religious, mystical and unreasoning past, and they
strove to combat them. In the fields of biology and medicine, for
example, a group of prominent scientists came together in common
opposition to what they feared were dangerous vitalistic trends
and declared their allegiance to science in what came to be known
as the Helmholtz School of Medicine. An 1842 statement by the
physiologist du Boise-Raymond captures the flavor: [6]

> Brücke and I pledged a solemn oath to put into power this
> truth, no other forces than the common physical-chemical ones
> are active within the organism; that, in those cases which can-
> not at the time be explained by those forces one has either to
> find the specific way or form of their action by means of the
> physical-mathematical method, or to assume new forces equal
> in dignity to the chemical-physical forces inherent in matter,
> reducible to the force of attraction and repulsion.

We see the strength of the commitment - a 'solemn oath' - and
the conviction that reduction to the content - 'physical-chemical
forces' - the methods - 'physical-mathematical method' - and
principles - 'forces of attraction and repulsion' - of physical
science was the only legitimate course. Brücke, a member of the
Helmholtz group, was the leading physiologist at the University
of Vienna, and Freud spent several years doing neurological
research in his laboratory. As Ernest Jones notes in his biography,
Freud spoke of Brücke as 'the greatest authority who affected
me more than any other in my whole life' (Jones, 1953-7, p. 25).
The direct personal influence of Brücke and the values he stood
for gave great force to this set of ideas and Freud was, early in
his career, powerfully taken with them. They left their mark on

many aspects of psychoanalytic theory.

THE EMERGENCE OF PSYCHOANALYSIS

While Freud was personally steeped in the values of science and
reason, and while his early life and career followed a conventional
professional and scientific course, there were, even during the
prepsychoanalytic period, other tendencies active within him –
sides that ran counter to rationalist-materialist values. He dabbled
with cocaine, went off to France to study hypnosis, and became
involved with Breuer and his new approach, his 'talking cure':
all activities on the fringe of respectable medical science. Throughout his life he read widely in literature, poetry and drama, was
drawn to Shakespeare and Goethe, to the study of history and
anthropology, and made increasing use of these sources in his
later work. And while he repeatedly chastised 'philosophers'
and other idle speculators, his late essays became quite speculative indeed.

The great turning point for Freud, both personally and pro-
fessionally, of course, was the creation of psychoanalysis itself.
One can trace a steady progression in his development of the
psychoanalytic method from its origins in the scientific world
view to its new form. Freud started as the objective scientist,
tracing neuronal pathways with the traditional microscopic
methods in Brücke's laboratory. He began his medical practice
and at first attempted to treat patients suffering from 'nervous
diseases' with physical methods: electrical stimulation, warm
baths, and the like. He was open-minded enough to see that these
methods – widely recommended by the medical authorities of his
day – had no lasting effects, and he initiated his collaboration
with Joseph Breuer, whose approach of letting patients 'talk out'
their problems seemed promising. Yet in this early work, the
patient was still treated as an object of medical manipulation;
hypnosis and suggestion were employed to 'remove' symptoms,
for instance. Freud's further development of the psychoanalytic
method took it further and further from its medical-scientific
origins. Hypnosis and suggestion were abandoned and the importance of the free flow of associations established. Much of the
work was directed at the analysis of impediments to the flow of
associations – with an increased understanding of the importance
of resistance, defense and anxiety. The complex nature of the
living relationship between analyst and patient moved to center
stage with the establishment of transference – and countertransference – as the core of analytic treatment. From an early, simple
view of therapy as the removal of symptoms – or the removal of
resistances and defense – analysis becomes, in its later, developed
form, the complex reexperiencing of the patient's life – and
especially of conflict-laden and poorly integrated early portions
of that life – within the confines of a specially constructed and
carefully nurtured human relationship.

It is not my intention to discuss the intricacies of psychoanalytic technique here; I have given this very brief description
simply to illustrate the transition from a medical-scientific
approach to a way of working with persons that is fundamentally
different. Freud created a method that defines - or embodies or
requires - a new paradigm, one not tied to the particular valuation of reason and objectivity, controlled observation and physicalist reductionism associated with the paradigm of science. Yet
this was not apparent, particularly in the early, creative transition period, and there was much mixing of terms and assumptions
as the new method took shape.

The transition in paradigms may be illustrated in yet another
way. During the years when Freud was developing the technique
of psychoanalysis, he also undertook his self-analysis, using his
own dreams as the primary vehicle. This represents a major break
with the objective and rationalist spirit of his day, which not only
viewed dreams as nonphysical, 'unreal' dross, but gave little
credit to an enterprise like a self-analysis. But for Freud himself,
the discoveries made in the self-analysis - an intrinsically subjective endeavor in which observer and object of observation are
one and the same person - were striking 'evidence' for the
validity of his new psychoanalytic propositions. He remained
convinced of the central power of the repressed Oedipus complex,
for example, not because he always 'found' it in his patients -
for it is by no means always clear in the case studies - but because he 'found' it within himself. I put 'found' in quotation
marks because the discovery is an act of self-interpretation that
has little to do with a scientific discovery such as finding a new
planet or isolating a new chemical element. Again, the point is
that this sort of discovery or truth is of a different character
than the discoveries and truths of science: it both comes from
and requires a different world view.

The new psychoanalytic method moved away from science in
many ways. Both the self-analysis and the psychoanalytic work
with patients immersed Freud in personal material - dreams,
neurotic suffering, anxiety, suppressed rage, masochism and
sadism, insanity, and the living versions of all these in the
transference - that made the traditional sort of scientific objectivity beside the point. A neurone under the microscope was an
object; so, conceivably, might be a physically ill person whom
one examines and treats with medicine or surgery. But the
weeping-raging-loving patient on the couch could not be objectified in the same way. And this was especially so as Freud
found the essence of the treatment to reside in the development,
understanding and interpretation of the transference. For to
work in this medium, the analyst must be a participant - not in
the ordinary way, to be sure; he does not 'act out' with the
patient - but his own feelings and associations must be sufficiently involved - there must be empathic understanding - in
order to effectively analyze the patient's transference reactions.
And, again, the point is that such work requires the abandon-

ment of the ideal of a rational, objective observer who is separated from the object of his scientific scrutiny.

THE UNFINISHED JOURNEY

We may now turn our attention to a brief consideration of the reasons for Freud's difficulty in making the transition from the conventional perspective to the new psychoanalytic world view. Why does the journey remain unfinished, even in his late work? I wish to suggest two sorts of reasons, one operating in the more or less conscious sphere, and the other having more powerful, dynamic or unconscious roots.

Along the line of the first, it seems always the case that any new discovery – any new scientific theory, philosophical system, religion, or approach to art, literature or music – shows the imprint of its origins. Even the most creative and original workers are influenced by those who precede them: Dostoyevski's early stories resemble Gogol's, Picasso's early paintings look like Puvis de Chavannes', the Beatles began by imitating Elvis Presley. So Freud's early works are well within the neurophysiological tradition of his day. The new work both shows the influence of predecessors and the imprint of the creative innovator as the old style, materials, or words are used in progressively modified ways. So we see Freud taking ideas and concepts from his neurologist past and reworking them into a new psychological theory: physical force becomes emotional force; neural, electro-chemical energy becomes libido or psychic energy; the barriers to transmission of nerve impulses become psychological resistance, and so on. Such carryovers of old terms are widespread in the creation of a new field and do not, in themselves, represent any unnecessary ambivalence or hesitancy about moving forward. One has to start somewhere – not even the most creative genius is born fully formed – and one typically reworks familiar materials and concepts that are ready at hand. If there are no other factors impeding the forward progress of the new work, the old terms eventually become understood in new ways. And this is the case with some of these transitional concepts in psychoanalytic theory: when one today speaks of 'resistance,' one refers to certain characteristics of the patient's mode of communicating – or not communicating – ideas, feelings and fantasies to the psychoanalyst and to himself. The fact that Freud originally took the term from a neurological model of the mind-brain in which it referred to the electrical 'resistance' that a nerve impulse encounters at a synapse is of only historical interest.

But there were much more powerful forces at work that made the transition from the old to the new world view a difficult one, forces that may be called unconscious. In part, these arose from the strength of the man-against-nature world view and the widespread acceptance and prestige of science and reason. To openly question these values would indeed put one in a lonely, isolated position. This was one reason why Freud was reluctant to sever his ties with science. And behind this, there was an even more potent issue – an issue that may be stated thus: using the new method of psychoanalysis, Freud found himself confronted with the horrible underside of civilization. Sexuality and love corrupted by guilt and anxiety; the mistreatment of children in the most respectable families; fathers seducing – literally and symbolically – their daughters; women taking revenge on their male oppressors in the way they treated their sons; separations, losses and deaths, so badly mourned, so incompletely dealt with; and insanity itself, with its terrifying pain and fear. The suffering of his neurotic patients – and his own neurotic side as he came to see in the self-analysis – bore a relation to the very 'progress' of civilization that so many outwardly extolled. What he discovered in the unconscious, in other words, could lead to a very critical – even a most radical or revolutionary – appraisal of his civilized society. To fully pursue the implications of these discoveries would have placed him in a very isolated position. It was one thing to be a doctor with a slightly odd new method, or even one who talked too much about sex – and psychoanalysis received plenty of criticism for this in the early days – but at least one could still claim to be a part of medicine and science. It would have been quite another thing to mount a criticial analysis of the dominant value system of one's society. Freud was quite hesitant about this latter course; he had little personal taste for it, as his letters make clear. Yet his ultimate honesty – and his persistence in doing psychoanalysis and remaining in contact with the evidence found in the unconscious – kept him moving in this direction, even though he clung to aspects of the old world view for support.

In sum, I think the primary reason for the failure to complete the transition from the old to the new perspective was that it was too revolutionary a step, implying, as it did, that the very virtues of civilization – of objective science, of reason, of progress – were directly implicated in the genesis of neurotic suffering. Freud eventually does state this – indeed we owe this crucial insight to him – yet he rarely says it directly or without qualifications and counterarguments.

Much more needs to be said about the complex interweaving of perspectives in Freud's work and, in the chapters to come, the main components of the theory will be considered in detail. But first, it will be necessary to discuss the question of the 'scientific' status of psychoanalysis at greater length. What does it mean to say that psychoanalysis is a science or to assert that it is not? If it is not science, as traditionally understood, what then is it?

3 PSYCHOANALYSIS IS *NOT* SCIENCE

Freud created psychoanalysis at the end of the last century in a world where science seemed inevitably linked with progress, with the transcendence of stagnant monarchal government, repressive religious authority, hypocritical morality, and superstition. It was not only his background in medicine and neurology, though these were important as specific sources, but these wider associations that led him to cast his theories in the form of scientific propositions, to cling to neurological models and terminology long past the time when psychoanalysis dealt with anything neurological and, in the most general way, to voice the belief – or hope – that psychoanalysis was a science. His search for the truth about human life, given the alignment of values of his time and culture, naturally drew him to science as the embodiment of progress and enlightenment.

Nowhere are these beliefs clearer than in the persistent way in which Freud opposes science and religion. From the early clinical papers that connected neurotic symptoms with guilt and repressive morality to such late works as 'The Future of an Illusion' (1927), science was associated with free thought and the possibility of human liberation; religion with the repressive authority of the Church and rigid moralistic strictures; science was tied to a mature, adult outlook, to facing life's realities with courage; religion with the escape into childish illusion and fantasy, with the wish for an all-powerful, fairy-tale father – God.

This opposition between science and religion captures certain important truths but, from our point in history, we may feel a bit uneasy with these old alignments. It hardly requires courage to call oneself an atheist in intellectual circles today, nor is one likely to be championing human freedom by urging a 'scientific' approach to the problems of psychology, society, politics or government. Indeed, in our secular age, this has become the establishment view; to say that psychoanalysis is a science, or that psychology, sociology, politics or history is – or should be – is to claim a certain legitimacy and respectability. Of even greater significance, it is no longer so easy to view interpersonal conflict, human misery and oppression as due to religion or superstition, or to champion rationality and scientific 'progress' as the solutions to life's difficulties. In our time, limitations on human freedom, the oppression of the individual and the stress that leads to neurosis and psychological pain may emanate from governments and institutions that identify themselves with rationality, material progress and the language of science more than from religion or other 'irrational' belief systems.

The fact that these alignments have shifted so radically since Freud's day is one reason to rethink the whole issue of the scientific status of psychoanalysis. Perhaps there are elements of childish fantasy in the hope that we can solve life's difficulties if only we are rational and logical enough; perhaps there are vestiges of magic and superstition in the repeated invocation of the word *science*, as in 'social *science*,' the '*science* of human behavior,' 'political *science*,' or the '*science* of psychoanalysis.'

I have chosen the provocative title of this chapter to point out the potential difficulties of the oft-heard claim that psycho-analysis is a science, a claim derived from an older system of values. I am convinced that a careful examination of psycho-analysis – both as a method of therapy and as a mode of theo-retical understanding – will show that it differs in crucial ways from what is typically understood as science. It does have some of the qualities of science, but is badly distorted by attempts to fit it completely within a scientific framework. Indeed, it has some of the qualities of religion and speculative philosophy – though Freud would be horrified to hear it characterized in those ways – but it cannot be equated with such fields.

If one thinks for a moment about Freud's discussion of science and religion, it should be apparent that he typically contrasts *scientific ideals* with *corrupt religious practices*. Modern critiques of science and rationality turn the tables; they contrast, for example, the *abuses* of scientific technology or the oppressive bureaucratic use of rational order, with humanistic or religious *ideals*. The pro-anti science debate is predetermined by these initial definitional alignments. Our first task in examining the relation between science and psychoanalysis, therefore, will be to clarify the multiple meanings and values that encrust the words in which this debate is typically framed: science, rationality, objectivity, subjectivity, and truth. With these clarifications established, we can then examine the several ways in which psycho-analysis has been tied to science.

In what follows, I will discuss the overextension of the world view associated with science and then examine the differing meanings of objectivity and truth in science and psychoanalysis. I will then take up the question of the place of general principles in the field, look at attempts to connect psychoanalysis with modern scientific models such as information theory, examine the role of bodily experience and, finally, look at the tendency of some psychoanalytic theorists to formulate sweeping explanat-ory dicta. As we work through these issues, our critical touch-stone will be the actual way psychoanalysis is conducted, both as a therapeutic-interpretive endeavour, and as a theory based on ob-servations from that endeavor. The critical survey will show that, while psychoanalysis shares features with science – as well as with religion, philosophy, and other areas – it cannot be adequately characterized in any of these familiar ways. Attempts to affiliate psychoanalysis with science may provide reassurance by association with prestigious and respectable social groupings, but it misleads one about the actual nature of psychoanalytic work. In a concluding section, I will offer some suggestions for a description that better fits the unique character of this work.

THE OVEREXTENSION OF THE WORLD VIEW ASSOCIATED WITH SCIENCE

For the past two to three hundred years - a period associated with the rise of science, the Enlightment, the Industrial Revolution, the decline in power of the Church and the coming into existence of modern states - influential thought in the West has moved steadily toward the scientific world view with its commitment to objectivity, rationality and physicalist explanation. Galileo against the Church authorities; Darwin's theory against religious fundamentalists; efficient new manufacturing methods against the Luddites; modern medicine supplanting prayer and superstitition: the lines of debate are well known. By the last half of the nineteenth century - certainly in intellectual circles - the scientific world view had carried the day. It was this view that so strongly affected Freud during the early stage of his education, perhaps most in the influence absorbed in the physiology laboratory of Ernst Brücke, an exemplar of the new science. (See Jones's biography for a discussion of Brücke's personal influence and Amacher, 1965, for an account of the role that Freud's neurological education played in shaping his later theories.) Most of us have been educated in this liberal-rationalist tradition, a tradition that embodies the victory of the scientific world view.

In recent years, a number of critical thinkers have begun to recognize that the world view of science may itself be overdone, that the very qualities associated with scientific progress in such fields as physics and chemistry may acquire the status of unquestioned dogma, especially when prescribed as guidelines for other fields.[1] What seems to have occurred is that the impressive triumphs of science led many to extend it ever more widely as a general approach to life's tasks. These extensions overemphasized those qualities that distinguished the scientific approach: objectivity, the use of reason, and the image of man as separate from a world of nature which he must master and control. In other words, the values, practices and images associated with science tended to become an ideology, a prescriptive system of belief, with no more 'scientific' foundation than any other ideology.

The ideology of science is bound up with an exaggerated version of certain of the qualities that are part of an actual scientific approach. Thus, where the separation of the reasoning observer from his emotions or immediate needs may be part of a practical and curious manipulation of the physical world, it is extended to a complex belief system which values reason over feeling, objectivity over subjectivity, the 'mind' over the 'body,' and which makes physical science and the controlled experiment guiding ideals for the social and life 'sciences,' for philosophy, the management of social and political affairs, and even for the mysteries of love and sex. *The problem is not with science itself but with the exaggeration of certain of its qualities and attempts to extend it in inappropriate ways.*

In point of fact, there are those who argue that this exaggerated ideology of science does not fit the work of physical scientists. Kuhn's well-known account of the role of paradigms (Kuhn, 1962) is one such analysis. In a related work Michael Polanyi states:

I start by rejecting the ideal of scientific detachment. In the exact sciences, this false ideal is perhaps harmless, for it is in fact disregarded there by scientists. But we shall see that it exercises a destructive influence in biology, psychology and sociology, and falsifies our whole outlook far beyond the domain of science ('Personal Knowledge,' 1958, p. vii).

One may or may not agree that detachment is a false ideal in physical science; certainly the best scientists are emotionally and personally involved with their work and use their intuition and feel for their subject matter. And there are several important ways in which work in modern physics requires an abandonment of the conception of a detached observer who is not a part of the phenomena he observes. Einstein's work in relativity shows how the observer must be taken into account as part of the phenomena being studied. Bohr's idea of complementarity – that it is impossible to separate the behavior of atomic objects from the instruments used to measure them – and Heisenberg's principle of indeterminacy – that one cannot determine both the location and velocity of an atomic particle because measuring one changes the other – both point to ways in which it is impossible to separate the observer from the observed. These developments in modern physics support analyses of science such as Kuhn's and Polanyi's which stress the impossibility of separating an 'objective' observer from his subject matter. The observer, with his paradigms, his predispositions, his instruments, is a part of the field of study. One can, in other words, find support for a critique of the ideology of science within the heart of science itself, though not all scientists are sympathetic with such efforts.

The strongest evidence for what Polanyi calls the 'destructive influence' of false scientific ideals can be found, however, in fields which take human life and institutions as their subject matter. Experimental psychology has been with us for almost one hundred years now, 'rigorously' aping the methods of physics and chemistry, and the fruit of these labors has been meager indeed. In fact, workers in this field seem to know more and more about methodology – about the correct way to be a scientist – and less and less about human life, supposedly the subject of their 'scientific' scrutiny. The same is true with attempts to scientize the study of politics, society, history, or ethics. What happens, all too often, is that a scientific-appearing approach in such fields

becomes a mask for the perpetuation of conventional values and
practice. By adopting the *form* of science, workers in these areas
engage in a kind of self-deception: they delude themselves, as
they attempt to convince others, that their work has nothing to
do with values, politics, ethics, or the authority and practices of
existing governments. In this way, the very scientific approach
associated with the search for truth has been perverted into its
opposite.

In sum: the scientific approach has been extremely valuable in
many spheres yet its very power and success has led to inappropriate uses and the extension of science to 'scientism.' The
attempt to fit psychoanalysis entirely within the mold of science
is such an inappropriate extension, in my view. Yet the issue is
a complex one, since psychoanalysis and science do have certain
characteristics in common, on the one hand, and since psychoanalysis does not fit within the mold of other familiar areas such
as religion or philosophy, on the other. In the sections that
follow I will attempt to explore both the connections and distinctions in some detail.

'Objectivity' and 'truth' in science and psychoanalysis
Objectivity and truth are valuable qualities in a variety of human
endeavours. While, for some, freedom from dogmatic authority
and the seeking after truth are synonymous with science, I think
we must recognize that these qualities are not the exclusive pro-
perty of any one field. One finds these ideals in law and government and in humanistic disciplines such as history and philosophy;
they are central to being a good teacher or parent, and one finds
them in art: the 'truth' or 'honesty' of a novel, a play or a poem.
Not all practitioners in these fields have been devoted to the truth,
have stood forth against ignorance and unjust authority, to be
sure, but neither have all scientists. And a rigorous pursuit of the
truth is essential to psychoanalytic work.

But there is a certain confusion that arises when the same word
– truth – is used with reference to these very different fields.
Truth in physical science refers to the accuracy with which a law
or principle fits observed phenomena, to the predictability of
hypotheses and the repeatability of observations and experiments.
In fields that take human life and institutions as their subject
matter, truth has more to do with personal honesty, with seeing
purposely obscured aspects of the self, of human relationships,
of families, governments and official ideologies. Honesty is a
crucial value in all these fields but personal honesty cannot be
equated with carrying out a scientific experiment in the prescribed
manner. It is more a matter of self-awareness, of cognizance of
the human tendency toward self-deception and egocentrism, of
the difficulty in striking a fair balance between one's own interests and the welfare of others. The avoidance of dogma and a
questioning stance toward authority are, similarly, crucial for
both types of truth, but for the second, this must include a
questioning of the dogma and authority of existing beliefs – includ-

ing the ideology of science.

The different meanings of truth can be seen in the contrast between 'scientific' truth and truth in psychoanalysis: *personal insight*. The ideology of science contains a set of assumptions for determining what is true – what is valid, repeatable, predict-able – which assumes that once such a truth is established, any-one can see it for himself; all he needs to do is look through the microscope under the appropriate conditions. But what is psycho-analytic truth? It is dependent on a form of self-knowledge, it does not exist 'out there' in the world to be apprehended by the detached observer. Rather, one arrives at it by a combination of introspection and interchange with other persons. The insights of psychoanalysis are apprehended by both patient and analyst through a back and forth series of communications, introspections and interpretations over the course of an analysis. The truths that emerge are forms of self-interpretation, changes in percep-tion and feelings about one's life, re-evaluation of memories and historical material, and shifts in how one acts with others. One can say that for patient and analyst alike, psychoanalytic truth or insight is akin to a paradigm shift and not like the accretion of information within an established paradigm, to use Kuhn's terms.

Just as truth can be understood in two different ways in psycho-analysis and models derived from science, so too, can objectivity. The ideology of science is deeply committed to the separation of the *observer as a person* from the subject matter being observed. This is sometimes referred to as the 'subject-object split' and it can be seen in a great variety of rules, values, beliefs and practices surrounding scientific work or the efforts of many in psychology and social science who attempt to identify themselves with physical science. In general it is assumed to be desirable, if not essential, for the scientific observer to keep himself as a person separated from his work. He must remain objective rather than subjective, approach his data in a detached, unemotional, unbiased manner, rather than be swayed by his predilections or feelings. The concept of control – with all its related methodology for data collection and analysis – arises from this assumption. Here, one operates in a manner such that the results of any well-controlled scientific study can be replicated by any investigator. Clearly, this emphasis on the importance of separating the personal qualities of the observer from his observations is a specific instance of the general attempt to extend the ideology of science to the study of human life.

This separation of the observer from the 'objects' being studied is inappropriate to psychoanalysis which studies persons, their thoughts, wishes, feelings, dreams, the way they live, why they are unhappy or have symptoms, how love develops, and hate, or guilt, the course of sexual pleasure and its many deflections and misdirections. We know these phenomena to one degree or another in ourselves and can learn about them in others by observing their behavior, by talking, asking, and listening to them describe their experiences, and by participating in various forms of

personal interactions, of which the psychoanalytic situation is
one very special sort. But who is subject and who is object – who
is observer and who observed – in all of this? The 'objects' of
such investigations are living human beings who observe themselves and their observers, think about both, and construct their
own 'theories' and hypotheses about what is going on. And from
the side of the designated observer, since we have no direct
access to the mind of another, we must continually use our own
correlated subjective experience to understand what is being
described. For example, a patient describes a dream. We cannot
see it but we construct our own version and, putting this
together with other things we may know about him from previous
communications and experiences in the living relationship – the
transference – we may offer an interpretation. The patient, in
turn, takes this and understands it in terms of his experience
and his previous work with the analyst. Does this resemble, in
any way, an astronomer observing stars through a telescope, a
physicist observing subatomic particles in a linear accelerator, or
a molecular biologist observing the outcome of an experiment?
Stars, particles and molecules don't observe the scientists who
observe them. They don't think or construct theories about us.
And we cannot 'know' them by empathy or partial identifications.
The subject-object split – the scientific ideal of the detached
observer – simply does not fit the study of human psychology and
psychoanalysis.

While the above examples have shown that scientific objectivity,
defined in terms of a detached impersonal observer, is inapplicable
to psychoanalysis, there is an important sense in which the psychoanalyst is objective. For while he must use his personal reactions
– his empathy, partial identifications, feelings of love, anger or
sexual arousal – as clues to what is going on in the interaction
with the patient, he must also remain partially removed from these
reactions. The term 'counter-transference' refers to the personal-
emotional reactions of the analyst to the patient and, in an ideal
analysis, one strives for awareness of counter-transference to
enhance the sensitivity of interpretations. One of the main purposes
of a personal or training analysis is to develop the analyst's understanding of himself so that he may effectively utilize counter-
transference reactions. But this is a disciplined use: one does not
express anger, love, anxiety or sympathy to the patient when one
feels them, for there is always the danger that the counter-
transference can swamp or seriously distort the analysis. Thus,
one important meaning of psychoanalytic objectivity is the effective
use of counter-transference reactions based on self-awareness.
And, while this overlaps in some ways with scientific objectivity,
it is clearly a very different process.

Let me conclude this discussion of the differences between
scientific and psychoanalytic truth and objectivity with an illustration that gives further evidence of the potentially distorting
effects of a misplaced scientism. Freud was fond of examples which
linked neurotic symptoms to religion. He showed how the rituals of

the compulsive were like the rituals of prayer and incantation
and how both could be understood as displaced struggles against
masturbation or as childish supplications to a parent figure. Many
of these insights remain extremely valuable in expanding our
understanding both of neuroses and religion, though most often
this is religion in its corrupted form and not the essential
religious impulse. That is to say, certain neurotic rituals are
caricatures of religion. But there are ways in which a neurosis
is also a caricature of science. Many neurotics suffer from an
over-objectification of some aspect of themselves; they treat
some part of themselves – their sexual organs, their angry
thoughts and feelings, their infantile fantasies – as the scientist
treats the object of his experiments: fractionating, isolating,
separating and ignoring surrounding qualities. In a sense, a
neurosis can be like a tightly defined scientific paradigm; it
makes sense of some narrowly defined set of phenomena while
ignoring much else. Of course there are crucial differences in
both purpose and outcome; I am not implying that scientific work
is 'neurotic.' But I am suggesting that it is the same human
capacity to separate – to split mind from body, reason from
feeling, objective from subjective, and conscious from unconscious –
that makes possible both the triumphs of physical science and the
neuroses of human individuals. Clearly, if psychoanalysis is
concerned with both understanding and treating neurosis, it cannot do so from within a world view that is deeply committed to
this very process of separation, that so values the subject-object
split. To state it in slightly different words: psychoanalysis
strives for wholeness, for integration, for making unconscious
material accessible to consciousness, for expanding the scope of
'the ego,' for widening the arena of the self to include repressed,
defended and split-off parts. It cannot do so from a world view
which is based on and values a particular form of separation.

The discussion to this point has covered ground that should
be familiar, at least to some. Criticisms of the misuse of science,
of subject-object separation, and of a false objectivity are not
novel. But, one can grant these criticisms and still attempt to
maintain a link between psychoanalysis and science. That is,
there are more sophisticated arguments for the connections
between the two areas, to which we must now turn.

The place of general principles in science and psychoanalysis
A sophisticated proponent of the scientific status of psychoanalysis
might present the following argument. He would agree that the
observer cannot be separated from his subject matter and that
physical science is an inappropriate model for psychology. Indeed,
he might cite the example of modern physics to show how the most
advanced scientists no longer hold with a subject-object split.
And he would agree with the various criticisms of how an ideology
of science has been misused. *But*, he would argue, there is a
more essential way in which science and psychoanalysis are
identified: both search for and formulate general principles.

Science is associated with the discovery and formulation of generalizations - principles, laws, theories - that make sense of diverse human experiences. If psychoanalysis is a discipline, a theory, a method of treatment - if it has anything to say about human life beyond the description of individual cases - it must also contain generalizations, such an argument would run. While these are not quantitative like the laws of physics or chemistry, they are principles, none the less and, therefore, psychoanalysis is a science. It formulates hypotheses or generalizations on the basis of empirical observations; these can be stated in a form accessible to other observers; and they may be tested by empirical methods. This is a more subtle argument, for I believe that there are both points of contact as well as crucial differences between the generalizations of psychoanalysis and the empirical principles or laws of traditional scientific fields.

Let me say, first, that there is no question that there are general principles within psychoanalysis, though there may be some disagreement among theorists as to what the central principles are. On the one side are those who have used Freud's meta-psychology - the version of psychoanalytic theory couched in a quasi-physical language of forces, energies, objects, and cathexes, - as the basis for a general theory. David Rapaport's - The Structure of Psychoanalytic Theory: a systematizing attempt - (1959) is one such effort and Rapaport and Gill's 1959 paper that outlines the various 'metapsycological points of view', another influential statement. While there are still those within the psychoanalytic fold who think a general theory can be based on the metapsychology, I believe that more and more are coming to recognize that efforts such as Rapaport's have proven relatively empty. The metapsychology does not hold up on its own terms as science - there are no clear referents for its concepts, it does not lead to testable hypotheses, it cannot be either verified or disproved - nor is it of much use clinically. Insofar as such efforts are tied to older conceptions of science, they are subject to the criticisms presented in the preceding section. There have been sufficient criticisms of this sort of theorizing by now that we need not review them here. [2]

Freud's writings contain a wealth of insights into the regular features of human behavior, regularities that succeeding genera-tions of psychoanalysts have confirmed in their work: that dreams give special insight into hidden areas of the personality; that neurotic symptoms, slips of the tongue, the mistakes of everyday life or peculiarities of character may be understood as metaphors - as symbolic statements - of central areas of personal conflict; that certain childhood experiences - especially involving sexual pleasure, and also key frustrations, traumas, threats and punishments - are connected to later neurotic and character problems; that intense experiences of conflict and anxiety are warded off - repressed or defended - yet continue to influence adult behavior from a level outside of consciousness. These are all examples of what can be termed clinical principles: generaliza-

tions based on psychoanalytic observations that are not tied to
the metapsyschology.

The late George S. Klein has presented the most detailed
version of what he terms the 'clinical theory' and this can serve
as a reference point for a general consideration of the status of
psychoanalytic principles. Klein (1976) attempts a systematic
definition of seven principles of the clinical theory, briefly:

1   That the personality (or 'psychic structure', in his terms)
both in normal and pathological development, results from the
resolution of *conflict*. Psychological growth occurs in response
to the confrontation of incompatible needs and aims and developmental crises. The theory assumes both a dialectical process
of change and also, the inevitability – indeed, the necessity –
of conflict.

2   That there is a striving for integration – for the resolution
of conflicting trends into wholes – and that this striving is
experienced as the need for a coherent *self*. This principle
relates to, but is also quite different from, what is known to
many psychoanalysts as 'ego-psychology.'

3   & 4   That experiences of *pleasure*, on the one hand, and
anxiety, on the other, are crucial determinants in the development of the personality and the structuring of motives. Klein
stresses the experiential aspects of pleasure and anxiety: the
first is associated with states of well-being, desirability, love
and connection; the second with estrangement, threat and
conflict.

5   That developmental crises and conflicts, especially those
heavily laden with anxiety, are repressed, dissociated or
split-off from the conscious self. This is the well-known
principle of *repression and the unconscious*: its effects are
seen in the many forms of defense, resistance, neurotic
character structure, and the like.

6   That the integrated ego develops through a process of
active mastery in which passively endured experiences and
traumas are actively repeated and become part of the self via
identification. The processes described in 5 and 6 are connected
to the second and third principles: experiences imbued with
great *anxiety* lead to *repression and dissociative splitting*,
those with a greater balance of *pleasure*, to *active mastery*.

7   That the conflicts encountered in adult life reactivate
earlier prototypes of conflict resolution of both the dissociative
and mastery type. This is the principle of *regressive repetition*,
necessary to explain object relations and transference in its
positive and negative forms, as well as other phenomena.

Whether these clinical principles are exhaustive or not remains
to be seen. My own feeling is that Klein has managed to draw
together the essential core of psychoanalytic thought in a very
clear way. The principles as he states them have a number of
valuable features. They are *developmental*, contain a central
conception of *conflict* – both inter and intra personal – and are
stated in a *language of human experience*. In addition, they

subsume a wide range of the phenomena observed by psychoanalysts and contained in the work of Freud and later theorists.
Some important areas - aggression, hostility, and their internal
versions as guilt and the conflicts of conscience - seem left out,
but they can be incorporated within the principles of conflict,
repression, and mastery. (For another, related attempt at a
summary of the principles of psychoanalytic theory see Loevinger,
1966.)

In sum, it is possible to extract general principles from the
common core of psychoanalytic observations. Does this mean that
psychoanalysis is a science? We can approach this question by
asking, 'how do these psychoanalytic principles differ from the
laws of science?' A central difference is illuminated by an issue
already discussed: the merger of subject and object, the inap-
plicability of a split between observer and observed. Put in
different terms, the 'data' for these principles is human experience -
a point that Klein repeatedly emphasizes (and that he only arrived
at late in his own work after he broke free of his experimental
psychology background). In this general way, there is never
anything *objective* that can be viewed under standard conditions
by interchangeable observers. Internal conflict, the coherent
self, experiences of pleasure and anxiety, repression, mastery,
and repetition occur within and between living persons and do
not exist apart from such contexts. The subject matter of psychoanalysis is intra- and inter-subjective. No observer can 'know'
these phenomena without the participation of the 'subject.' This
is one crucial way in which psychoanalytic principles are distinc-
tive from the generalizations of other scientific fields.

A second difference also involves the inherently subjective -
or perhaps one should just say 'psychological' - character of the
field. Because of this there is an inevitable looseness to the
principles. The principles themselves are not akin to laws; they
are not and never will be predictive in any precise way. They
are more in the nature of *guidelines*: they tell the psychoanalytic
observer where to look as he works with his patient. What is
more, such work is not a scientific enterprise, not an experiment
nor even the postdictive effort one finds in geology or astronomy.
It is a collaborative exploration of the meaning of a life, an
exploration motivated by pain and dissatisfaction, whose goal is
a realignment of personal meaning and experience. A full understanding of principles of the sort just described rests on insight
into oneself. In other words, one only knows about repression,
anxiety, or transference repetition when they are experienced in
oneself, as well as observed in others.

The argument that psychoanalytic principles are not much like
the laws or theories of science does not minimize their significance. From their long immersion in the collaborative efforts of
psychoanalytic work, together with a continuing exploration of
themselves, the best workers in this tradition have built on,
modified, and refined Freud's ideas. We know a good deal about
the general results of certain sexual, interpersonal, and traumatic

experiences of childhood; we are able to recognize – from clues, dreams, and partial evidence – general configurations of character and their associated conflicts; we know a good deal about the ebb and flow of anxiety and defense, of progress and resistance, of dissociative splitting and mastery. There are, in other words, a number of established and communicable aids to finding one's way around in the unconscious and the transference-countertransference. But such general guidelines or aids are only loosely predictive. And the work of psychoanalysis does not consist in making them more precise – more valid or exact – as one does with scientific hypotheses. Rather, such work involves the explication of the meaning of an individual life as lived and experienced. In a sense, every particular psychoanalysis can be thought of as the creation of a personal paradigm with the principles as general guides, rather than as the predictive application of such principles or the testing and refinement of scientific hypotheses.

In summary, psychoanalysis, both in practice and theory, involves the exploration of personal-subjective meaning, an exploration that uses general ideas or principles derived from previous experience as guides on a creative-exploratory journey. [3]

'Modern' scientific models in psychoanalysis
There is yet another way of linking psychoanalysis with science, a way proposed by those with a sophisticated appreciation of the limitations of older scientific models. Those engaged in such efforts argue that the problem with Freud's version of a scientific psychoanalysis was its connection with an outmoded neurology and its commitment to mechanistic principles such as those of the Helmholtz program, a program which attempted to limit psychology to physical entities subject to the laws of attraction and repulsion, conservation of matter and of energy. If one takes these commitments literally – and Freud himself never did, he always used the physicalist language metaphorically – it is extremely difficult to deal with mind, thought, purpose, wish, goal-directed action and the social nature of life: in short, with the subject matter of psychoanalysis or psychology. Different solutions have been proposed for this problem. One has been the attempt to banish the mental entirely – to restrict the field to observable behavior – the way of behaviorism from John B. Watson to B. F. Skinner and his current followers. The less said about these misguided efforts the better. Another was by abandoning science entirely for some 'phenomenological' or 'existential' version of psychology.

But the development of cybernetics, computers and what is now generally known as information theory provides a different alternative, a way that seems to resolve the conflict without giving up either one's commitment to science or the core of the psychological subject matter. For work in information theory has shown that one needs concepts such as purpose, goal-direction and 'thought' – as in plans, schemas, or programs – in order to account for the behavior of such clearly mechanical things as thermostats, guidance devices, and computers, and that information theory provides a valuable model for physiological systems like those regulating body temperature and blood chemistry, the operation of the brain and nervous system, and much more. In other words, here was a modern form of science on which to 'base' psychoanalytic theory much as Freud attempted to base it on nineteenth-century biology. [4]

What is one to make of these efforts at modernization? I believe there have been some valuable contributions arising from the use of these new conceptual models but also a continuation of the old problems stemming from a misguided attempt to appear 'scientific.' In the examination of these issues, I will draw examples from adjacent psychological fields as well as from psychoanalysis itself.

Older scientific-mechanistic theories - both in psychology and psychoanalysis - faced two general problems: (1) the difficulty of accounting for purposeful action and, (2) the problem of the context-dependent nature of behavior. According to the tenets of a mechanistic or physicalist-behaviorist approach, the concept of 'purpose' - of human action that is determined by its goals - is teleological and, hence, unscientific. Explanations in terms of purpose were likened to saying a rock falls to the ground because it 'wants to,' which explains nothing in a scientific way about the behavior of falling objects. In psychology this issue was at the heart of the old debate between behaviorists and cognitivists and, while behaviorism has achieved a certain popularity in recent years, the arguments and evidence were on the side of the cognitive theorists from as early as the 1930s, if not before. Aside from such uninteresting phenomena as knee-jerks and eye-blinks, little of human behavior can be explained without taking into account the 'internal' or 'mediating' process of the person: his thoughts, plans, goals, and purposes. If psychology needed a way of encompassing such internal process, psychoanalysis needed it even more. For those in both fields who wished to identify themselves with science, information theory was greeted as an ideal solution to this problem.

The second major problem for older scientific approaches was the context-dependent nature of human action. In the traditional science ideology, there was a great emphasis on the separation of phenomena into discrete entities which could then be studied under controlled conditions. 'Behaviors,' 'responses,' 'operants' were to be the psychological counterparts of atoms and molecules. While not as abhorrent as teleology, the idea that 'things' are different in different situations - that the whole is *more* than the sum of its parts as the Gestalt psychologists used to say - was deemed unscientific. But psychological 'things' are different in different contexts. Within psychology, there have been numerous demonstrations of the determining effects of context, background, paradigm and schema, from the early perceptual demonstrations of the Gestalt psychologists through the work of Piaget and his followers. This great mass of evidence makes clear that human actions cannot be understood or explained as discrete entities apart from a context which defines their meaning.

Just as information theory seemed to rescue purpose and goal-directed action for a scientific psychology, so general systems theory was seen as a modern scientific solution to the problem of the context-dependent nature of action. Systems theory – which is closely tied to information theory, often the two coexist in the work of the same author – brings in the notion of the *interacting system* from biology, engineering and other clearly scientific fields. For example, modern neurophysiology finds it cannot meaningfully study the firing of single neurons without taking into account the reverberating fields of surrounding neural activity. One must, in other words, consider the functioning brain as an *integrated system*. As another example, work in the Darwinian-naturalistic tradition stresses the process of *species adaptation*, in which one must consider both the characteristics of the animal and the features of the surrounding ecological niche as a total interacting system. These, and many other examples from engineering, ethology, medicine and biology, all provided instances of a 'scientific' use of context-dependence.

Now, what can be said about the use of ideas and models from information and systems theories in attempts to renovate and modernize psychoanalysis? First, that some work of real value has come from these efforts and, second, that there has been a pull back towards a false scientism. As examples of the first trend let me briefly discuss Bowlby's work on attachment and Bateson's views on schizophrenia.

Traditional psychoanalytic theories of human infancy pictured the infant as a discrete or independent creature, impelled into action by internal drives such as orality or the pleasure principle. The mother was similarly viewed as a more or less independent being who, because of the socialization that had been imposed on her, learns to care for her baby. Bowlby (1969, 1973) criticizes this theory and presents an alternative model which he constructs from ethology, information and systems theories, as well as from observations of mothers and infants. In his view, mother-infant attachment is an evolved, adaptive system that unfolds during the first year of life. Action within the system is regulated by the transfer of information between mother and infant – smiles, nursing, holding and related actions – which propel both toward the achievement of the preset goal: attachment. Bowlby works out this conception in great detail, including reactions to separation, the place of anxiety and the coordination and differentiation of his ideas from others in psychoanalysis, but here is not the place to discuss all that. I cite his work as an example of how *general* information and system conceptions have been put to valuable use in this sector of psychoanalytic theory.

In a related way, a number of recent workers, of whom Gregory Bateson (1956; see also 1972) was one of the first, use information and systems ideas to illuminate the problem of schizophrenia. In many traditional accounts, the schizophrenic was considered a discrete individual, his mental illness or psychological disturbance viewed as a thing within him. Bateson and others ask us to view the schizophrenic as part of a system: his family. And when one is able to do so, what were before unintelligible signs of illness often become understandable components of a bizarre family communication pattern. As was true of work on mother-infant attachment, research on family systems and schizophrenia is a large, complex and controversial field that we need not review here. Whatever its ultimate contribution will be, I think many would agree that it is an instance of the way in which ideas from information and systems theory have sparked extremely valuable contributions.

In sum, conceptions from information and systems theories have been useful as models for purposeful action and for taking account of the context of human action. They allow us to view persons guided by their goals and ideals and give models – the programs of computers – for the complex cognitive structures that underlie language, thought, and imagination. In a more general way, these modern approaches show that human beings are not like atoms or billiard balls – are not independent, un-thinking, unpurposeful entities or objects bouncing around between stimuli, libidinal energies or the forces of attraction and repulsion. But here a paradox becomes evident. For there is a sense in which everyone knew this all along; we are all aware of the importance of purpose, thought and plan in deter-mining action, and the model of an isolated entity hardly des-cribes the real life of anyone. It was the dictates of a particular science ideology that led such concepts as purpose or context to be stigmatized in the first place. One is then forced to rely on a more modern version of science to legitimize them. One should not have needed either old or new science – and many sensitive observers did not – to appreciate that mothers and infants are an interacting dyad, as the model of attachment holds, or that certain unfortunate creatures are driven crazy – and kept that way – by their families, as Bateson's model of schizophrenia proposes. So while these new versions of science have been productive in some instances, part of their value has lain in correcting the mistakes created by a science ideology that was, in the first instance, inappropriate to human life.

There is, as well, a tendency for the underlying ideology of science to reassert itself, even in those fields where information and systems conceptions have made valuable contributions. Thus, where the early work on the role of the family system in schizo-phrenia was very suggestive, the reaction of the scientifically oriented has been to 'scientise' it: the focus has been on the 'systems' side of 'family systems'; there are attempts to 'tighten up' the model, make it more testable, give its terms operational definition, and formulate methodological critiques of those who work in an experiential way with these ideas.

One finds a reassertion of the ideology of science in modern versions of a scientific psychoanalysis as well. This often takes the form of replacing the terms and models of a nineteenth-century machine with those of a twentieth-century computer. While this

may be a more felicitous analogy, it is still an escape from the
realities of human experience; in the long run, the basic assumptions of the ideology of science are retained as human experience
is objectified in this new language of 'information', 'programs',
'bits', and 'feedback loops.'

Psychoanalysis, science and the 'body'
There is another argument for tying psychoanalysis to science,
specifically to biology, medicine, physiology and related fields
which contain important information about the functioning of
the human body. A proponent of this position would point out that
psychoanalytic work reveals the great importance of the body,
of body symbolism and of early experiences of pleasure and pain
associated with certain body zones - oral, anal, and genital.
Related work in the psychosomatic field shows the interconnec-
tions of 'mind' and 'body,' of the many ways in which psychological conflict relates to and is expressed through physiological
disturbance. Do not these connections argue in favor of giving
psychoanalysis a 'solid biological base'? Is it not crucial to have
an understanding of the physiological processes involved in
psychosomatic disease? Won't we be better able to work with all
the physical-bodily manifestations of conflict when we understand
them scientifically? How is one to understand these issues and
answer these questions?
    The place of the body in psychology and psychoanalysis can be
approached in two quite different ways. One of these ways is
part of the general world view of which traditional science is a
part: it represents a continued attempt to fit the study of human
life within the framework of science. The second approach, which
is consistent with the essence of psychoanalysis, treats bodily
phenomena in quite a different fashion. Whether work with 'the
body' is useful to psychoanalysis or not depends on which of
these two paradigms it comes from.
    When workers operating from the paradigm associated with
science speak of giving psychoanalysis a base in biology they
usually mean that one should study some psychophysiological
problem - say stomach ulcers, migraine headache or sexual
impotence - with the methods and concepts of biology. Thus,
one studies the secretion of stomach acid, variations in blood
supply to parts of the brain, or levels of adrenalin during
sexual arousal. One may learn a good deal about the operation
of such physiological processes, but the value of such knowledge is limited, for in practice such work almost always moves
away from the personal, meaningful and social aspects of bodily
or psychosomatic conditions. It moves in that direction because
it is done within a paradigm which leads one to separate bodily
functions from their context and study them as independent
'variables.' For workers in this tradition, such separation is
crucial for a controlled, objective and, hence, scientific approach.
Such work focuses on the transmission of nerve impulses, the
biochemistry of hormones or neurotransmitters, the permeability

of cells; it can tell us much about the functioning or mal-
functioning of the body as a machine but, because it exists on
a 'split' and objectified level of discourse, it never tells us what
any of these processes mean to a particular person in his life.

Let us look at an example that will show the difference between
such a scientific approach to the body and the approach I think
is more consistent with psychoanalysis. Suppose someone loses
a leg in an accident. This is clearly a biological-bodily event
and one likely to be of great significance in the individual's life.
But to understand that significance, we will need to study what
the loss means to him, and this can only be done by examining
what sort of a person he is, what his past experiences were that
prepared him in one way or another to cope with the trauma, who
is available in his current social world and how they respond,
and so forth. Studies of such events show a rather amazing range
of human response. The physiology of the leg loss is a part of
all this, and it would be important to know whether an infection
developed, or structural damage caused continued pain, but these
'biological' factors would only be parts of the larger picture.

Psychoanalytic understanding of the body is more like the
understanding of the social-psychological response to loss of a
limb than it is to say, the physiology of migraine headaches or
stomach ulcers. Its level of discourse starts with the person and
his subjective experience and expands outward to include his
social world, rather than reducing downward to biological science.
The central examples of bodily phenomena that psychoanalysis deals
with all illustrate this. We see that the earliest sense of self or
ego is constructed from bodily sensations, feelings, actions and
such key interpersonal experiences as feeding, being held,
comforted or, on the other side, feeling frustrated, abandoned,
and in pain. Such experiences are the basis for a symbolism of
the body that continues into later life in the form of posture,
movement, facial expression, and is expressed in later verbal
and imagistic forms. Let us consider an example that illustrates
how the body and bodily experience is understood within this
psychoanalytic framework.

Picture an infant who is deprived of love, attention and adequate maternal care during the first years of life. Initially, this
results in a deprived-depressed orientation to persons and can
be observed in a depressed facial expression, low levels of
activity, and the excessive reliance on substitute objects of
gratification such as thumb-sucking, soft toys, rocking and
other forms of self-stimulation. As an adult, some of these bodily
manifestations - such as the depressed look - may persist, while
others undergo forms of symbolic elaboration. Thus, the thumb-
sucking may vanish to be replaced by a preoccupation with food,
diets, and body weight. The early, behavioral aspects of deprivation - the seeking of physical contact with maternal figures - may
be transformed into a complex personal psychology in which human
relationships are viewed in terms of giving and getting - though
instead of food and physical contact, the focus might be on praise,

success, or money. Even with the tremendous symbolic elaboration
that is typical in such cases, a core of bodily-emotional experience typically remains, perhaps manifested in sensations of being
'filled-up' after a big meal or filled with the sensations of sexual
pleasure, on the one side, or never being satisfied no matter
how much food or sex is consumed, because of the persistence
of the early feelings of deprivation, on the other. This example
shows that bodily phenomena are often quite central but only
as they arise in an inter- and intra-personal context, only as
they are symbolized and given meaning in the course of an
individual's life. This complex process of development, experience, social response, symbolization, and transformation exists
on a different level of theory - it is part of a different framework
of understanding - than the body of biological research.

Searching for the psychoanalytic laws of gravity
Consideration of the relationship of psychoanalysis to science
has taken us down a long and somewhat tortuous road. We are
near the end - the attempt to state what psychoanalysis *is* if it
is not science - but I must beg the reader's indulgence as I
consider one final issue before we reach that goal. This may be
thought of as reductionism and the search for certainty within
the psychoanalytic framework itself. The early form of this is
seen in Freud's own quest for the big unifying concept, the grand
principle that unites a broad group of observations. He first did
this with sexuality, later with the pleasure principle and finally
with the large polarities of libido-aggression, Eros-Thanatos and
life-death. Underlying these concepts is a search for something
like the psychoanalytic laws of gravity, principles to which the
diversity of human experience might be reduced.

Many psychoanalysts after Freud have fallen prey to this
reductive trap. For example, it has been common to take the insights that connect neurotic and character problems to specific
psychosexual stages - oral, anal, oedipal - and to elevate them to
the status of law-like explanatory principles. Erik Erikson describes the penchant that psychoanalysts have for 'originology' -
the tendency to explain all of adult functioning in terms of its
infantile origins. At its worst, this leads to a procrustean form
of analysis where each patient is forced into some stereotyped
formula. For Freud and his immediate followers, the Oedipus
complex was sometimes used in this way; later, other patterns
have been employed in a similar fashion. For example, a number
of the followers of Melanie Klein seem to take her insights concerning the place of depression and aggression in infancy and
make of them formulae for explaining almost everything in every
patient. The problem is not with the insights - which may be
quite cogent when applied to certain persons or certain spheres
of experience - but to the way in which they are used with such
finality as reductive explanations. Using psychoanalytic insights
in this way is a temptation that the practicing therapist must
guard against: it is the danger of viewing the individual patient

as *just another instance* – of the oedipal complex or whatever –
rather than using the theoretical principle as a guide in unraveling the meaning of his particular life.

In short, it is possible to work wholly on a psychological level,
to deal with symbolism and meaning, to abandon the quasi-
physicalist metapsychology, to not seek a false legitimacy by
connection with other fields of science, old or modern – to remain
solidly within the boundaries of psychoanalysis itself – yet to
fall prey to reductive practice and the search for certainty. While
these sins are not exclusive to those who attempt to scientize
psychoanalysis they do, it seems to me, derive from the general
world view associated with science. And they are incompatible
with what psychoanalysis is all about.

We have surveyed the general features associated with the
world view of which science forms a part and have considered,
as well, a number of ways in which psychoanalysis, both in
practice and as a theory, does not fall within that view. Throughout this discussion have been scattered some comments regarding
how psychoanalysis may be defined once one abandons the claim
that it is, or should be, a science. It remains to tie these together
in a concluding statement.

WHAT PSYCHOANALYSIS *IS*

There are two interrelated aspects to the question 'what is psychoanalysis?' The first has to do with *subject matter*, and the second
is a delineation of *method*, of how the subject matter is to be
approached. I would urge that we be 'scientific' – empirical – in
specifying both subject matter and method; that is, that they be
primarily defined by what occurs in the process of psychoanalysis
itself. This process consists of a particular kind of introspective
communication (free association – or approximations to it) in a
specially constructed interpersonal situation (the analyst-patient
relationship) that facilitates the observation and interpretation
of the patient's characteristic personal-emotional patterns (transference). As I have argued earlier, this collaborative work is
guided by principles derived from much previous psychoanalytic
experience but can never be objective, precise, controlled or
predictive as the physical sciences are. The subject matter is
comprised of the observations and inferences – interpretations
and insights – that analyst and patient arrive at as a result of
their work together in the psychoanalytic setting.[5]

The collaborative work of patient and analyst over the course
of an analysis can result in a description of personality or
character structure. This includes conscious and unconscious
components and such central phenomena as: the ego or sense
of *self*; the many dispositions (or 'structures'), identifications,
sets and attitudes – including the central areas of masculinity
and feminity and their related qualities – that are the outcome
of a developmental history; the characteristic ways one has

developed for dealing with conflicts - sexual, aggressive,
dependent - that form the prototypes activated in present encounters with related conflicts; and one's dissociated, repressed,
or disavowed sides, active in relation to anxiety, depression,
guilt, and other painful affects and memories. All of this may be
thought of as constituting a *personal paradigm* - a term I will
introduce here to refer to the subject matter of a psychoanalysis,
and that will help in the discussion of method that I now wish to
pursue.

One develops a personal paradigm over the course of life in
a specific family-social context. The extent to which one is
conscious or unconscious of this paradigm may be thought of as
the degree to which it fits one's life experience. In other words,
a personal paradigm may be more or less complete, may encompass
a little or a great deal of one's experience, and may be flexible
or rigid, open to modification and change or relatively fixed.
The person, in other words, may show shifting degrees of conscious and unconscious qualities. When we say someone is 'neurotic' - where major portions of his experience are unconscious -
we mean that he lives by a narrow and rigid personal paradigm,
one which does not change when exposed to new events, but
which continues to react to current situations in terms of earlier
prototypes. While some of the words in this definition are new,
there should be little quarrel with its overall form, for it simply
recasts familiar psychoanalytic concepts in a slightly different
language.

*The essence of the psychoanalytic method is the exploration
and understanding of personal paradigms*. In an actual analysis,
patient and analyst are engaged in an exploration of the patient's
personal paradigm as this is lived and experienced in the therapeutic situation. The goal of this exploration is a form of personal
knowledge, understanding, or insight. The most difficult and
time-consuming part of this process involves those anxiety-laden
areas that are actively disavowed: the well-known unconscious
conflicts with all their tenacious defenses and resistances and,
therefore, 'making the unconscious conscious' - a goal of psychoanalytic work - is a central part of the understanding of the
personal paradigm by which one lives one's life. This way of
defining the analytic method may be coordinated with two other
well-known versions: Freud's dictum 'where id was there shall
ego be,' and the broader idea that the goal of psychoanalysis is
insight. If we define the ego as the conscious part of the personality - the part that includes awareness and self-reflection - and
the id as all that is unconscious, then Freud is saying that
analysis allows one to bring sides of oneself - those id-related,
impulsive, conflicted, unsocialized sides - within the view of a
conscious and reflective self. It does not do away with the id,
it does not 'cure' in the sense of taking away the patient's
disease; instead it enables one to see old issues in new ways, it
permits an expansion or change in personal perspective. The
same may be said about insight, the general goal of psycho-

analytic work. When one achieves insight into a previously
repressed side of oneself, one has expanded the scope of a
personal paradigm; one has, in other words, discovered a form
of personal truth – however unpleasant – and accepted it as
one's own.

I will not attempt to coordinate this definition of method with
the intricacies of psychoanalytic technique, though it must be
stressed that personal paradigms are not abstract, intellectual
affairs; they are manifested in characteristic interpersonal
relationships and involve the strongest of feelings. Thus, one
can only get at them in situations where some intensity of
personal-emotional contact is possible. Psychoanalysts speak of
the ideal interpretation, and the insight that results from it, as
touching on three areas: the transference, current life relationships, and events from the past. When this sort of insight is
achieved, the person can experience some aspect of himself as
he is feeling and thinking it in the relationship with the therapist
(transference), *and* see how these reactions derive from the past
he has been reexamining, *and* how they relate to the repetitive,
unresolved conflicts in his current life.

In the most basic sense this kind of insight allows one to
become aware of the *consequences* of living in accord with a
'neurotic' personal paradigm. One comes to see how, let us say,
the anxiety and guilt connected to childhood sexual experiences
are continually reexperienced in current relationships and how
one defensively attempts to avoid such feelings with symptoms,
inhibitions, or a particular style of sexual encounter – say a
perversion. As all of this is brought to light, one experiences
the limitations imposed by an old, rigid pattern – limitations in
freedom of action, ability to feel, or scope of relationships. And,
having seen all this – experienced it live in the therapeutic
relationship, understood something of its genesis, and recognized
how one continues to repetitively reenact it – one is then free to
change. But that is not quite correct: one cannot engage in a
deep process of self-exploration such as this without changing;
the commitment to the process is a form of change in itself.

Psychoanalysis should be conceptualized as a uniquely new
endeavor: a field devoted to the exploration and understanding of
personal paradigms from a *metaparadigmatic* position. By meta-
paradigm I mean that in order to explore and understand a
paradigm, one cannot remain wholly within it. The method requires
that one move to a position of *neutrality* where there is a greater
openness to multiple points of view. Since the stuff of analysis
is personal and subjective, it can only be known by experience,
the analyst cannot be totally abstracted from the material being
analyzed, he must know it to some degree on the basis of first-
hand contact. But he must, at the same time, not be so committed
to his own version of things – his own paradigm – that he is
unable to explore and understand that of the patient.

Ideally, the psychoanalytic enterprise is carried out from such
a position of neutrality and openness. One strives to see the

value of reason and feeling, of male-heroic and feminine-receptive
qualities, of social conformity and revolutionary change, and of
the many specific attitudes, values, ways of loving, working and
raising children that comprise the spectrum of human life. No
real psychoanalyst – not even a Freud – can achieve such an
ideal. He who is truly open with regard to his patent's sexual
orientation may have an unexamined bias in favor of work as a
good in itself; he who is very open to revolutionary social ideas
may unthinkingly overvalue certain modes of child rearing.
Neutrality, openness, the valuing of multiple truths, different
life paths for different persons are ideals, always imperfectly
realized in any actual instance.

   In sum: psychoanalysis is *not* a science, though it shares some
of the qualities associated with a scientific approach – the search
for truth, understanding, honesty, openness to the import of
new observations and evidence, and a skeptical stance toward
authority. It is an art, similar to other complex applied arts such
as medicine, architecture, law, government, literature, or drama,
but also very different from all of them. It is a kind of psychology,
though quite different from many approaches that currently bear
that label. It is, despite Freud's protestations, a philosophy, a
system of values, and an approach to life, though also very
different from many philosophical and religious systems in the
West. It is, in short *psychoanalysis*, a unique discipline which I
have attempted to define as the exploration and understanding of
personal paradigms from a metaparadigmatic position.

4 THE THEORY OF SEXUALITY

Freud's insight into the role of sexual factors in neurosis was
one of his great early discoveries. The first forms of psychoanalytic treatment were aimed at uncovering sexual traumas
and, from the beginning, the general theory posited sexual
force as a primary motive in human life. From these early roots
Freud later developed the broader theory of infantile sexuality
and this, in turn, led to that appreciation of the formative
importance of childhood emotional experiences of many kinds
that we now take for granted. In the broadest sense, psychoanalysis helped bring about large changes in our conceptions
of sex, masculinity and femininity. It is part of the twentieth-
century change in consciousness that includes the liberation
from old taboos and guilt-inducing restrictions, the reappraisal
of the meaning of pleasure, and a marked shift in the treatment
of sex and play in infancy and childhood: in short, changes
in the most basic ways we think and feel about childhood, our
bodies and our identities as males and females.

Freud and psychoanalysis can rightly claim a central role in
the criticial reappraisal of all these areas; yet, paradoxically,
within psychoanalytic theory itself, sexuality is treated in
ambiguous and inconsistent ways, reflecting the unfinished
journey, the incomplete transition from a conventional to a
critical world view. This can be seen in the mixture of positive
and negative feeling and value in writings that concern sexuality.
It is described as the most powerful of human motives, and is
frequently related to neurotic sickness, perversion and symptoms
while, at other times, it is exhalted as eros, the energy of love,
the great binding and cohesive force of civilization. And then,
again, it is pictured as the infantile pleasure principle, manifested in selfish, narcissistic and antisocial forms. The pleasure
principle itself is treated in a most contradictory way in the
major theoretical work devoted to it, 'Beyond the Pleasure
Principle' of 1920, where it is simultaneously tied to the forces of
life and of death! These contrasting images illustrate the coexistence of value and feeling arising from the two different
perspectives.

Within the conventional world view, the sexual side of human
nature is felt as an enemy, as a dangerous temptation, as a
threat to man's strength and sense of self. The sexual strictures
of the Judeo-Christian tradition, the prudery of Victorian society,
and such specific nineteenth-century beliefs as the virtues of
female chastity or the destructive effects of autoerotism all

51

illustrate this trend. In addition to expressing condemnation of sex, such views are male-centered: women, and the feminine side of men, are connected to the dangers of sexual pleasure. Sexuality as eros, its association with life, procreation and the forces of love arise from a very different world view. Conceptualizing sexuality in one of these ways or the other leads to crucially different appraisals of its role in neurosis and other forms of psychological disturbance. Thus, one can 'blame' neuroses on the sexual instinct *or* one can see them arising from the specific familial and social structurings of sexuality. In the first instance, one feels human beings are possessed of a dangerous, rapacious force that can only be kept in check by the strongest of countermeasures. Life is a continuous struggle between this antisocial instinct - the id - and the controlling forces of civilization - the superego. The best we can hope for are less malignant compromise formations. This view is consistent with, indeed arises from, the nineteenth-century European conception of sexuality and the feminine. And this was, necessarily, Freud's starting place. *Or* one can view sexuality as malleable and open, its expression shaped in quite different ways in different persons, families and societies. Within this second view, neurosis arises from the particular way sexuality is treated: the timing, form and nature of taboos, frustrations and traumas. This is the view contained in the theory of psychosexual development. And this second position leads, inevitably, to a *critical* appraisal of the dominant society's conceptualization of sexuality and such closely related topics as masculinity-femininity, motherhood and the treatment of children, and the general dialectic of work-discipline versus play-pleasure. [1]

The psychoanalytic theory of neurosis contains both conventional and critical views, in shifting mixtures, as we will see in the next section. The metapsychology, Freud's attempt to translate his findings into a general theory, presents a different version of the problem. There, the conventional view of sex is disguised in an abstract theoretical language which obscures its origins and the persistence of conventional assumptions. The problems with the metapsychological version of sexuality will be examined in the following sections, which trace the historical development of sexuality in psychoanalytic theory. Finally, the examination of several of Freud's case studies of women will allow us to explore the inconsistent treatment of female sexuality.

SEDUCTIONS, SEXUAL FANTASIES AND THE PRIMAL SCENE

There is a more or less standard account of Freud's discoveries of the role of sexuality in neurosis which tells of the shift from a seduction theory to one focused on the impulses and wishes of the patient. Freud did, at one time, believe that neurosis originated in actual sexual traumas - that his patient's memories of seduction in childhood (most frequently girls by their fathers)

were true. As he reports in 'An Autobiographical Study' (1925),
he became skeptical that so many respectable parents could have
seduced their children and later came to believe that the seductions had never taken place but were fantasies made up by the
patients. As he puts it:

> I was at last obliged to recognize that these scenes of seduction
> had never taken place, and that they were only fantasies which
> my patients had made up or which I myself had perhaps forced
> on them.... I was able to draw the right conclusions from my
> discovery: namely, that the neurotic symptoms were not related
> directly to actual events but to wishful fantasies, and that as
> far as neurosis was concerned psychical reality was of more
> importance than material reality (1925), p. 34).

As Freud goes on to show, this shift in theory led to several
major advances in psychoanalysis: the broader conception of
infantile sexuality (countering the prevalent belief in childhood
innocence), the discovery of the *Oedipus complex* (a more sustained interpersonal drama than a simple trauma or seduction),
and the significance of *psychical reality*. Yet, as is so typical
in Freud's work, this shift to new modes of thought also perpetuated certain conventional assumptions. For example, there
is the revolutionary insight into the enormous role of fantasy
in everyone's life. Psychical reality must be recognized, memories
are *constructions* of the person, not literal or photographic *re-
productions*. What is more, they are constructions strongly shaped
by wishes, fears and conflicts. Freud's emphasis here, along with
the recognition of the central role of fantasy, is on *the symbolic
transformation of experience*. The move beyond the simple trauma
theory was part of this shift to a psychological level of analysis
with an awareness of the complex interplay of conscious and unconscious factors. But, in a sense, Freud went too far, for while
childhood memories are constructions that are colored by wishes
and symbolically transformed to reduce anxiety and pain, they
are not wholly creations of the patient. They are based on actual
experience, and the nature of this experience is crucial to the
genesis of neurosis. We all live a good part of our lives in fantasy,
yet this fantasy is, necessarily, a symbolic transformation of our
'reality.' Yet it is here that the wish theory takes a conventional
turn, for Freud sometimes writes as if the fantasies arise entirely
from the child. Where the trauma theory put the blame on seducing
parents – a strong indictment, indeed, of respectable society –
the wish theory shifted the culpability back to sexuality itself,
which now, behind its various disguises, appeared more devious
than ever. Thus, the important recognition of psychic reality
became confounded with a retreat to a conventional view of a disruptive sexual instinct.

It was another aspect of the conventional world view – the
commitment to dualistic assumptions – that made it difficult for
Freud to formulate an integrated account, one that gave due
weight to both actual experience and to fantasy. Freud often
writes as if it must be one or the other: either neurotics have

been traumatically seduced or it is all a product of their imaginations - imaginations fueled by rapacious sexual instincts. From a
nondualistic perspective we would say that neither sexual instinct
nor reality exist apart from each other. Reality is a construction
of the perceiver, including the reality of sexual instinct and
experience. Sexual fantasies and impulses *and* the family-social
milieu interact to shape a neurotic course of development. From
this viewpoint, neurotic symptoms are the *symbolic transformations* of childhood experiences involving sexual impulses *and*
parental response (seductions, desertions, betrayals), all within
a social-historical context. This is the version of the role of
sexuality in neurosis that can be drawn from the theory of psychosexual - or as Erikson puts it in 'Childhood and Society,' one of
the clearest accounts of the theory, 'psychosocial' - development.
Within that theory, the balance of pleasurable and painful experiences with key persons at crucial stages of development - oral,
anal, oedipal - are the prototypes for later sexual-emotional
disturbances of a correlated form. Sexuality is understood in the
broad sense of experiences involving pleasure and pain in various
body zones within typical interpersonal stages: feeding-attachment-
orality, discipline-anality, and sex-role identification-oedipal.
This theory does not limit the childhood events that cause
neuroses to the strictly sexual; experiences of death and loss,
rejection and abandonment, physical illness, violence and other
forms of mistreatment are known to play their parts.

The broadened theory of psychosexual-psychosocial development completes the transition in world view begun by Freud when
he moved from the trauma to the wish theory. It is, essentially,
a 'symbolic transformation theory of neurosis' which gives a
central place to the traumas of early life - for no one becomes
seriously disturbed without them, though they are certainly not
restricted to seductions or to sexuality - and to the imaginative
and otherwise active participation of the person who becomes
disturbed. [2]

Let us now examine a specific sexual trauma, one that clearly
illustrates the persistence of conventional assumptions: the
primal scene. From early on, Freud believed that the child's
observations of his parents engaging in sexual intercourse was
always traumatic. More than that, he postulated that the child
would tend to give a sadistic interpretation to his parents' sexual
activities, envisioning the father as aggressor and the mother as
victim, and identifying with one or the other. Even if the child
did not actually see his parents engaged in sex, he might hear
them in the bedroom at night or simply construct fantasies from
his observations of animals and these fantasies, like the sight
of the 'scene,' would be sadomasochistic, traumatic and anxiety-
producing. Now it should be clear that these ideas grow directly
from conventional nineteenth-century views of sexuality as evil
and dangerous. Even the *sight* of it - or the *thought* of it - is
enough to frighten an innocent young child, especially a
virginal young girl! I suspect that little credence would be given

to such an idea today if it were stated in these bald terms. Yet clothed in psychoanalytic garb, and backed by Freud's authority, this anachronistic idea has remained a staple of orthodox analytic theory. (See Esman, 1973, for an excellent critical review of the primal scene in Freud and a number of later writers.)

Many of the young women described in 'The Studies on Hysteria' were supposed to have been traumatized by the sight of sex. Freud bases a major portion of his analysis of the Wolfman (in Freud, 1918) on the trauma that this patient presumably suffered at age one-and-a-half when he observed his parents engaged in anal intercourse. In my view, the explanation of the Wolfman's pathology in terms of the primal scene trauma is extremely strained; it is perhaps the least satisfactory of all Freud's speculative case constructions. The Wolfman's own account, as well as much later material (see Gardiner, 1971) points to much more sustained and powerful sources of early trauma. Both of the Wolfman's parents were seriously disturbed, perhaps even psychotic, and they came and went - both physically and emotionally - in an erratic manner throughout his childhood. He probably suffered a severe physical illness at a young age, and was cared for by at least five substitute mothers of varying quality (see Blum, 1974 and Peck, 1979). The Wolfman's disturbance was serious and long-lasting and I think many experienced psychoanalysts would feel that such a condition can hardly be accounted for by the sight of parental intercourse, at whatever age and in whatever position. That certain images or fantasies connecting the sight of parental sex with anxiety may have remained as symbolic referents for larger and more complex childhood traumas is certainly possible. But this is not Freud's hypothesis of the traumatic effects of the scene.

It is curious that the primal scene hypothesis has persisted for so long since it is so culture-bound, so clearly an inappropriate generalization of European middle-class values. In most primitive, most peasant, and many nonwestern cultures, where children have ample opportunity to observe the sexual activity of adults, they are not routinely traumatized by such experiences. So in this sense, the literal version of the primal scene hypothesis reflects the persistence of conventional views of sex as a harmful activity. But there are other ways of viewing the same clinical material, ways that stem from a critical perspective. Perceptive psychoanalysts recognize that it is never the sight of sexual relations *in themselves* that are traumatic. Thus, in his careful review, Esman concludes that 'evidence that observation of parental intercourse is per se traumatic to the child is not convincing; certainly, no specific pathological formation can be ascribed to it' (1973, p. 76). He goes on to note that 'sadistic conceptions' of the scene, as these are seen in the child's fantasy and symptoms, result from 'overt violent aggression' in the parents' treatment of the child, not from simply observing sex. In addition to direct aggression, clinical experience reveals a great variety of ways in which parents impose inappropriate

sexual demands and stimulation on their children: lonely, depressed mothers who turn to their young sons for love and sexual
stimulation, fathers who take out the frustrations of their lives
by molesting their daughters, or families in which all sorts of
bizarre sexual rules are imposed on children in the name of
virtue and morality (see Laing and Esterson, 1964, for examples
of this last). In all these instances, the sexual conflicts of
parents are transmitted to children, setting the stage for their
conflicted conception of sex; there is, in other words, a transmission of sexual guilt, anxiety and conflict from one generation
to the next. It is this sort of complex family-social experience
that makes sex traumatic, and not the sight of the primal scene
per se.

When one examines sexuality – and such related areas as
masculinity-femininity or the autoerotic activities of childhood –
in this way one moves toward a critical appraisal of society. One
cannot, for example, honestly investigate sexual sadism and
masochism apart from the social values which defined males as
dominant and placed women in positions of inferiority and sub-
servience. In contrast to such a socially informed view, the
idea that the sight of sex is in and of itself traumatic, that it
gives rise to anxiety and sadistic fantasies, has remained for
so long in psychoanalysis because it is politically safe. Like the
metapsychological conception of a disruptive sexual energy, the
primal scene hypothesis deflects attention from the interpersonal
and social experiences that make sex frightening rather than
pleasurable for some persons or that connect intercourse with
aggression or masochistic suffering.

What is true of the primal scene is true of other sexual experiences of childhood: they become traumatic – they become connected
with anxiety, guilt, and neurosis – by virtue of their specific
treatment within a family and society. In summary : traumas,
whether single events like a seduction, or the more complex
experience of an oedipal complex, may be viewed from two perspectives, one conventional and the other critical. This same
mixture of perspectives exists in other parts of psychoanalytic
theory, particularly in the metapsychology, as we will now see.

FREUD'S EARLY THEORIES OF SEXUALITY

The persistence of conventional assumptions in the metapsychology
is a complicated and subtle matter which can best be approached
by tracing the historical course of Freud's theories of sex and
the sexual instinct. We may begin with his early ideas as they
are found in his correspondence with Wilhelm Fliess (Freud,
1887-1902).

The Fliess letters and drafts are revealing in a number of
ways. Freud is struggling to make sense of the various neuroses –
the complex somatic and psychological conditions displayed by
the patients that came to him. He is still much influenced by his

earlier work in neurology and there is the attempt to write a
'psychology for neurologists' - 'The Project for a Scientific
Psychology' - which he works on with fits of enthusiasm and
despair, and eventually abandons short of publication (indeed
we only know of it through the survival of the Fliess correspondence). Along with the attempt to describe his psychological
findings in the neurological-reductive language of 'The Project',
Freud is continually inventing and modifying various other
hypotheses and theories and attempting to test them against his
clinical observations. He is still caught up with various medical-
psychiatric diagnostic schemes and organizes some of his
hypotheses around them as categories: 'anxiety neuroses,'
'hysteria,' 'neurasthenia in women,' 'neurasthenia in men,'
'mixed neuroses.' It is also apparent from the drafts and comments
sent to Fliess during this period that his own evaluation of his
developing hypotheses was shifting and uncertain. He could not
tell - as indeed who could? - which would become the corner-
stones of psychoanalysis and which would be dropped by the way-
side. Let us examine two of these developing lines of thought
which receive much discussion in the Fliess papers, one that
illustrates a progressive-critical and the other a regressive-
conventional trend.

The first is the theory of inner conflict and defense, elaborated
in 'The Studies on Hysteria' (1895) and in several key papers of
this period; the second is sexuality, its relationship to anxiety
and its role in neurosis. Here are some quotations from a discussion of defense from a draft on paranoia sent to Fliess in 1895:

Now it is in fact the case that chronic paranoia in its classical
form is a *pathological mode of defence*, like hysteria, obsessional
neurosis and states of hallucinatory confusion. People become
paranoic about things that they cannot tolerate - provided
always that they have a particular psychical disposition.

And, later in the same draft:

So what she was sparing herself was the self-reproach of being
a 'bad woman'. And the same reproach was what reached her
ears from outside. Thus, *the subject-matter remained un-
affected*; what was changed was something in the *placing* of
the whole thing. To start with it had been an internal reproach;
now it was an imputation coming from outside. The judgment
about her had been transposed outwards: people were saying
what she would otherwise have said to herself. Something was
gained by this. She would have had to accept the judgment from
inside; but she could reject the one from outside. *In this way
the judgment, the reproach, was kept away from her ego* (Freud,
1887-1902, pp. 109 and 111. All italics in original).

This, it seems to me, is as clear a statement of the basic conception of defense as Freud is ever to make. The major neuroses, he
indicates, are pathological variations of the normal psychological
processes by which persons keep from themselves - from consciousness, from their image of an acceptable self - intolerable
'reproaches' and impulses. The specific discussion of the paranoid

woman delineates projection in a manner that we would find acceptable today. And the discussion of other patients, in material from this period, treats similarly the sexual impulses of hysteria, the guilt and self-reproaches of obsessionals, and related clinical conditions. This theory will require much further work, of course. It lacks a developmental scheme and the idea of the internalization of key relationships - the superego - is yet to be stated. But all that will flow quite directly, as will many other aspects of psychoanalysis concerned with conflict and modes of conflict resolution. This basic early theory, and the later formulations that will be built on it, moves in that direction I have termed criticial, for Freud's examination of internal conflicts involving the self and guilt ('self-reproach' in the quoted passage) will eventually take him to an examination of the role of civiliza- tion in the creation of neurotic conflict.

Side by side with the theory of defense are Freud's developing ideas on the role of sexuality in the neuroses. And if the theory of defense is clear, progressive and critical, the speculations concerning sexuality are inconsistent, shifting and mixed together with the conventional sexual prejudices of the era. Freud has made an important discovery: the correlation of something in the sex lives of his patients with their neurotic symptoms. The problem is in specifying just what the sexual factors are and in pinning down the interrelationship of sex, anxiety and neurotic symptoms. For a correlation or coincidence of factors is not the same as a causal relationship. It is in his attempts to specify the sexual factors and delineate the direction of causality, that Freud falls back on conventional prejudices which saw children - and women as well - as asexual and potentially traumatized by exposure to sex, which looked with horror on autoeroticism of all kinds and, indeed, which seemed to stigmatize all forms of sexuality other than 'normal' coitus between married adults. Thus, there is much speculation in the letters and drafts about sexual *noxa*, about the harmful effects of coitus interruptus, about sexual exhaustion leading to *neurasthenia*, about masturbation in child- hood and adolescence setting the stage for adult neurosis, about the 'sexual traumas' that innocent young women suffer when they get married (he reminds Fliess to keep these letters and drafts away from his young wife), and about the long-lasting and damaging effects of sexual pleasure - seductions - in early child- hood. In some cases it seems that too much sexual stimulation is the problem; in others it is inappropriate timing; and in still others it is incomplete sexual release. But all these explanatory schemes rest on the idea of a dangerous instinct which must be carefully channeled into a narrow form of acceptable expression lest severe disturbance result.

The relationship of sexuality to anxiety is a closely related problem where a clear correlation is observed, but in which conventional prejudice obscures the development of a sound theory. Anxiety and the many ideas, actions and symptoms related to it, is widely observed in the neurotic patients. But

Freud's major hypothesis at this time is that anxiety is a secondary symptom; it results from sexual stimulation that is not discharged in the 'normal' or adequate way. *Thus, where the theory of defense sees guilt and self-reproaches as the cause of defense and symptoms, this model sees anxiety and related symptoms as the results of improperly expressed sexuality.* And where the first theory breaks fresh ground and prepares the way for the great psychoanalytic insights to come, the second interjects conventional prejudicial views of sexuality and women into psychoanalysis where they remain, under various guises, for a very long time.

SEX IN 'THE STUDIES ON HYSTERIA': THE EARLY META-PSYCHOLOGY

Freud, as both curious investigator and physician concerned with the treatment of the deeply disturbed patients seen in his neurological practice, was drawn to Breuer's account of his work with 'Anna O.' Anna, the first psychoanalytic patient, was seen by Breuer between 1880 and 1882. Her treatment consisted chiefly of talking things out – what she herself called 'chimney sweeping' – a method which appealed to Freud both as a potentially effective therapy (it is the forerunner of the cathartic method and free-association), and as a rich source of information to use in unraveling the mysteries of the psychoneurosis. He began his collaboration with Breuer on a series of cases and persevered alone after Breuer gave up the work, developing psychoanalysis as method and theory in the succeeding years.

'The Studies' is an extremely rich source of observations, ideas and hypotheses. When one reads it from today's vantage point, one can discern the embryonic form of many later psychoanalytic concepts, including: inner conflict, repression, defense, the unconscious, the role of childhood experiences in adult disturbance, the symbolic expression of unacceptable aspects of the self, and over-determination. These brilliant new psychoanalytic ideas coexist with conventional notions about the harmful effects of masturbation, the 'innocence' of young women and the generally threatening quality of sexuality. These critical new ideas and their conservative-regressive counterparts are mixed together in various blends throughout 'The Studies.' For example, the 'somatic' symptoms confront Freud and Breuer with a version of the mind-body or psychological versus physical causation dilemma. There are several ways of handling this, but for the most part, 'The Studies' takes a dualistic or 'split' position. This is one example of the perpetuation of a conventional bias even as a new insight is developed. In a more general way, various new lines of explanation are explored in the first chapter and in the case studies. However, in the final chapter, authored by Freud alone, a general theory is put forth, a theory that begins to solidify around conventional assumptions. This theory is developed into

the metapsychology proper in Freud's books and essays written
during the next twenty-five years. The metapsychology, as we
will see, remains a repository of disguised conventional assumptions about sexuality. Yet, during this development, other trends
are kept alive in the style with which the metapsychology is
written – the particular way Freud weaves other strands into
even the most mechanized theory. Let us trace this Janus-faced
development of theory from its starting place in 'The Studies.'

In the jointly-authored first chapter (On the Psychical Mechanism of Hysterical Phenomena: Preliminary Communication), Freud
and Breuer present their initial theory of neurosis. Hysterics
have experienced 'traumas' at earlier points in their lives and
the effects of these traumas remain active. 'Hysterics suffer
mainly from reminiscences' (S.E., vol. 2, p. 7 – all further
quotations from 'The Studies' are from that source), they state,
because the normal processes by which the effects of trauma
would be dissipated have not occurred, or have in some way been
blocked. Here is how they put it:

> The fading of a memory or the losing of its affect depends on
> various factors. The most important of these is *whether there*
> *has been an energetic reaction to the event that provokes an*
> *affect*. By 'reaction' we here understand the whole class of
> voluntary and involuntary reflexes – from tears to acts of
> revenge – in which, as experience shows us, the affects are
> discharged. If this reaction takes place to a sufficient amount
> a large part of the affect disappears as a result. Linguistic
> usage bears witness to this fact of daily observation by such
> phrases as 'to cry oneself out' and to 'blow off steam'. If the
> reaction is suppressed, the affect remains attached to the
> memory. An injury that has been repaid, even if only in words,
> is recollected quite differently from one that has had to be
> accepted (original italics, p. 8).

This quotation captures the essence of the theory, yet so many
possibilities, so many different lines of inquiry could move out
from it. 'Trauma' could – and does in the example cited at this
point in 'The Studies' – encompass the whole gamut of painful,
unhappy and frustrating human events. 'Affect,' as the quotation itself illustrates, may include anger and sadness (crying)
and, in later discussions, sexuality and all the emotions related
to it. And the notion of discharge of an affect in an appropriate
or normal direction opens the whole realm of social and cultural
variation, for the 'normal' way to express anger, sadness or love
is always defined and limited by social mores, rules and taboos.
While these many lines of thought are suggested, they are not
all followed at this time. A consideration of social-cultural factors
comes much later, as does a differentiated model of the stages of
child development.

The early theory of neurosis assumes that there are normal or
healthy reactions to 'traumatic' events. In the examples quoted
above, these would be to cry or to 'blow off steam' – to express
anger. When this healthy reaction is blocked, the affect is kept

alive in a dammed-up form. The trauma, along with its associated complex of ideas, continues to exist in a 'split-off consciousness' (an obvious early version of the unconcious). The treatment developed in accord with this model stressed the recovery of the forgotten trauma and the release of the blocked affects and associated ideas. This was principally in the form of a verbal-emotional outpouring – 'catharsis,' 'abreaction' – to the physician who maintained a sympathetic interest in the patient.

In discussing the curative effect of catharsis, they state: 'It brings to an end the operative force of the idea which was not abreacted in the first instance, by allowing its strangulated affect to find a way out through speech . . .' (p. 17). Here the key phrases are 'operative force' and 'strangulated affect.' Action is impelled along some course or channel by a 'force' associated with 'affect' and when (for reasons largely unspecified in 'The Studies') this course is blocked, a state of 'strangulated affect' leads to, or causes, neurotic symptoms.

We can note several things about this model before discussing Freud's further elaboration of it. First it is stated in terms derived fairly directly from the clinical work, and rests on observations available to the shrewd student of human behavior. When a loved person dies, the normal reaction is to cry; when one is insulted, to lash back in anger. If one reacts in these ways the affects or feelings eventually spend themselves. The neurotic does not do this, so in this sense he is driven by pent-up feelings. The examples and terms in 'The Studies' are close to human experience: affect, trauma, memories, ideas – even the new technical terms catharsis and abreaction have clear referents in 'crying oneself out' or 'blowing off steam.' It is also important to note that a number of affects or emotional states – crying, sadness, anger, revenge, love, grief and mourning – are all implicated in the genesis of neuroses.

To sum up: the preliminary theory stresses the role of trauma (presumed real events) and undischarged or unexpressed affects and their related ideas. It is stated in a psychological (as opposed to metapsychological) language, whose terms are taken directly from human experience (love, anger, revenge, grief) or are easily translatable to such experience (catharsis, abreaction). What does Freud do with this theory?

First, he keeps it. As was characteristic of his style, Freud develops new theories without giving up the earlier ones, which are left scattered throughout his writings like the archeological remains of a prior civilization. In this respect, his theories are like the unconscious in his famous analogy with the city of Rome, the various layers from past to present all coexist (see 'Civilization and Its Discontents,' p. 29). I point out this feature of Freud's thought before discussing the main structure of the metapsychology he was erecting in order to alert the reader to the fact that these substructures coexisted from the beginning.

While a theory stated in a language of psychological experience, and encompassing a variety of affective or emotional states, appears

in various ways in later writings, the metapsychological version
of the theory moved in a different direction – a direction in which
*sexuality comes to stand for all affects and psychological-
experiential terms are replaced with physicalist-energic ones.*
Thus the metapsychology is reductionistic in two separable ways:
(1)   various affects and emotions are all subsumed under sexuality or libido; and (2)   there is an attempt to reduce psychological-
experiential phenomena to a language of physical entities and
energies. In addition, the understanding of what is perhaps the
crucial experiential aspect of neurosis – *anxiety* – gets side-
tracked into a theoretical quagmire where it remains for thirty
years. Let us follow these developments, beginning with the
treatment of anxiety.
    In the final chapter of 'The Studies' Freud begins with the idea
of blocked affect but soon modifies this in a way that both retains some of its original meaning while altering it in the direction of a general, sexual-libidinal energy. A typical quotation:
    Thus, starting out from Breuer's method, I found myself
    engaged in a consideration of the aetiology and mechanism of
    the neuroses in general. I was fortunate enough to arrive at
    some serviceable findings in a relatively short time. In the
    first place I was obliged to recognize that, insofar as one can
    speak of determining causes which lead to the *acquisition* of
    neuroses, their aetiology is to be looked for in sexual factors
    (p. 257).
    Anxiety appears at many points in 'The Studies.' It was clear
to Freud that many of his patients' symptoms were connected
to states of fear, fright and dread. In the early discussion,
he treats anxiety on the same experiential level as the other
affects. But he treats it quite differently in the final chapter
when he is constructing the causal theory. There, anxiety is
seen as the result of blocked sexual discharge. For example,
Freud discusses 'anxiety neurosis' in which symptoms or equiva-
lents are '*manifestations of anxiety*, . . . [that] arise from an
accumulation of physical tension, which is itself once more of
sexual origin' (p. 258). There follows a discussion in which
various features of the neuroses – phobias, hyperanesthesia to
pain, hypochondria, obsessional ideas – are all brought within
a common framework: *anxiety as blocked sexuality*. A discussion
of the cases follows in which the sexual root of each patient's
hysteria is emphasized. Frau Emmy von N.'s anxiety and phobias
'originated from sexual abstinence.' Miss Lucy R. was 'an over-
mature girl with a need to be loved, whose affections had been
too hastily aroused through misunderstanding.' 'Katharina was
nothing less than a model of what I described as "virginal
anxiety".' As we saw in the earier consideration of the Fliess
correspondence, Freud has observed a *correlation* between anxiety
and disturbed sexuality that can be interpreted in at least two
ways. In constructing his theory he chooses to see anxiety as
the result of 'blocked' or 'abnormal' sexuality, an idea consistent
with conventional views of sex. The alternative is to see the

anxiety as prior – to see the disturbance in the sexual lives
of his patients as a result of childhood experiences in which sex,
bodily pleasure and love have become connected with anxiety,
guilt and 'self-reproaches.' This second view is certainly 'psychoanalytic', and we even see an early form of it in 'The Studies.'
But it is not the view that Freud used in the metapsychology;
indeed, it only finds a clear place in theory thirty years later
with the publication of 'Inhibitions, Symptoms and Anxiety' (1926).

Let me emphasize once again that many trends – progressive
and regressive, revolutionary-critical as well as conventional –
all coexist in Freud's work of this period. Sexuality is, of course,
a central aspect of love – especially when taken in its experiential
rather than physical-discharge sense – and the patients in 'The
Studies' show serious disturbances in their sexual-love relationships, as most neurotics do. Freud's focus on these, and the use
of his new theory of inner conflict, defense and the unconscious
to illuminate them, is the beginning of the revolutionary psychoanalytic mode of understanding. Another great insight is the
connection he makes between neurotic disturbance in adult life
and experiences in childhood. Here he opens up a crucial area:
the symbolic transformation of experience. At this point it is
the idea that a 'sexual trauma' from the past can be symbolically
expressed in a symptom, a phobia for example, or in a symbolism
of the body – loss of sensation, paralysis, or peculiar pains.
Many of the psychoanalytic works in the immediately succeeding
years are elaborations and extensions of this seminal idea. The
theory of dream symbolism, treated at length in what Freud considered his greatest work, 'The Interpretation of Dreams' of
1900, begins with the model of neurotic symptoms as symbols of
inner conflict. Dreams, Freud argues, are also symbolic transformations of central conflicts. In a related way 'The Psychopathology of Everyday Life' of 1901, and 'Jokes and their Relation
to the Unconscious' (1905c) rest on the same essential idea. We
should also note that in all three of these works, the conflicts
that find their expression in symbolic form are not solely sexual.
Aggression, pride, revenge, fear, guilt, envy, embarrassment:
a number of emotions and 'drives' are implicated in the unconscious conflicts that gave rise to the dream, slip of the tongue,
or joke. But when he comes to treat these same matters in the
metapsychology, the multiple motives of inner conflict are replaced by sexuality and the idea of symbolic transformation is
replaced by the theory of the discharge, and blocked discharge,
of sexual energy. [3]

The emergence of physicalist reductionism can be seen in
Freud's final chapter of 'The Studies' where the conception of
sexuality passes from a language of experience to one of *libidinal
energy*. This reductive transformation goes hand-in-hand with his
solution to the problem of how sexual factors are related to
neuroses. For if, in the earlier discussion, the direction of the
correlation was not clear, the dominant idea here is a concrete,
nonsymbolic, or physicalistic one. It is, as well, a conception that

perpetuates conventional sexual prejudice. Symptoms are caused
by excessive sexual arousal in childhood, masturbation, and
other forms of sexual-sensual gratification. Similarly, dammed-
up sexuality due to abstinence or coitus interruptus is assumed
to produce anxiety – in the colloquial sense of 'nervousness' –
and related symptoms. In his paper –Sexuality in the Aetiology
of the Neurosis–, published three years after 'The Studies,'
when he has developed a more recognizable psychoanalytic
technique and was working on 'The Interpretation of Dreams,'
he still holds this concrete view. He begins with a long argument
in which he counsels physicians and others to overcome their
reservations and deal more openly with sexuality which is, after
all, a natural, biological function. But as the argument proceeds,
a view which is both conventional and nonsymbolic dominates:
> Masturbation is far commoner among grown-up girls and mature
> men than is generally supposed, and it has a harmful effect not
> only by producing neurasthenic symptoms, but also because it
> keeps patients under the weight of what they feel to be a dis-
> graceful secret. . . . If physicians knew that all the while
> the patient was struggling against his sexual habit and that he
> was in despair because he had once more been obliged to give
> way to it, if they understood how to win his secret from him,
> to make it less serious in his eyes and to support him in his
> fight against the habit, then the success of their therapeutic
> efforts might in this way well be assured (S.E., vol. 3, p. 275).

In the discussion that follows, Freud's stance with regard to
sex is again clear. It is a normal or natural function, and nothing
to be ashamed of, *only* in a very restricted sense: one assumes
heterosexual relations between adults. Masturbation in children
or adults, arousal without 'normal' consummation, abstinence, all
produce symptoms. This quotation illustrates the persistence of
nineteenth-century sexual prejudices – that one must fight
against the evil habit – but Freud's own words are open to another
interpretation – that is not the physically dammed-up sex, but
the *meaning* of the sexual activity (the feeling that sex is 'a
disgraceful secret') that is central to neurosis. And indeed, this
was a course that he increasingly took in his later work, though
not always so. Let us now turn our attention to these later
developments.

SEXUALITY IN PSYCHOANALYTIC THEORY AFTER 1900

The first of the 'Three Essays on the Theory of Sexuality' (1905b)
presents a very careful discussion of homosexuality and perversions in which Freud's awareness of cultural variations in the
definition and determination of these phenomena, and the many
subtle factors involved in their genesis and maintenance, is quite
striking. This shows Freud at his critical best, not trapped by
conventional assumptions. But the ambivalence – the contradictory treatment of sexuality – does not disappear in the post-1900

works, for despite the balanced treatment in the first section of the 'Three Essays,' the later portions give way to theorizing which not only reduces all affects to sexuality but which attempts to reduce a number of human actions to this source as well. Thus: 'it is easy to establish, whether by contemporary observation or by subsequent research, that all comparatively intense affective processes, including even terrifying ones, trench upon sexuality – a fact which may incidentally help to explain the pathogenic effect of emotions of the kind' (p. 203). The examples cited in this later section of the 'Three Essays' attempt to demonstrate the sexual root of a variety of emotional and behavioral states including fear, curiosity, muscular activity and intellectual work. Thus,

> In school children dread of going in for an examination or tension over a difficult piece of work can be important not only in affecting the child's relations at school, but also in bringing about an eruption of sexual manifestations. For quite often in such circumstances a stimulus may be felt which urges the child to touch his genitals, or something may take place akin to nocturnal emission with all its bewildering consequences (p. 203).

And, more generally,

> Finally, it is an unmistakable fact that concentration of the attention upon an intellectual task and intellectual strain in general produce a concomitant sexual excitation in many young people as well as adults. This is no doubt the only justifiable basis for what is in other respects the questionable practice of ascribing nervous disorders to intellectual 'overwork' (p. 204).

Similar arguments are advanced for muscular activity; that is, children engage in it as a substitute for sexual pleasure or because of the hidden pleasure they derive from it, and for pain which, again is linked up with sexual excitement.

These examples contain some brilliant psychoanalytic insights, of course. Intellectual work, looking, and curiosity more generally, may all become *sexualized* and so participate in neurotic symptoms and conflict. Similarly, some phobias, or the seeking of pain characteristic of certain masochistic persons, involve sexual conflicts in very intense and important ways. But, in the examples just cited, Freud goes far beyond this. He argues that *all* affective processes are sexual, and the examples and discussion clearly show the development of theory in which one motive force – sexuality – lies at the base of a variety of activities that are seemingly motivated in other ways. The other affects – anxiety, anger, fear, grief – present in the early discussion, have all been relegated to secondary positions, with sexuality the primary motive force.

A theory which attempts to explain so many human actions and feelings solely in terms of sexuality creates more problems than it solves. To illustrate this, let us look at an example of *sexualized looking* from one of Freud's own case studies, namely 'Notes upon a Case of Obsessional Neurosis,' (1909). In addition to the case as originally published, Freud's daily notes are now available and these throw important light on the connection between sex-fear-guilt and looking. The Rat Man suffered from a great number of sexual inhibitions, compulsive acts and rituals, obsessive thoughts and fears. Central to his disturbed state was the horrible image, which he could not get out of his mind, of a torture in which rats are placed on a victim's buttocks and bore their way into the anus. He kept thinking that this torture would be visited on certain of his loved ones. How does Freud make sense of all this? One way is by understanding the inhibitions in his patient's sex life: the Rat Man was rarely able to consummate sexual relations; indeed it was difficult for him to even touch women. He was more involved with thoughts and ideas and with looking, which had acquired a strongly sexual flavor. Thus Freud notes: 'but there was never mutual contact but only looking and at most pleasure from it. Looking took the place of touching for him' (p. 309). Freud's notes in the analytic hour immediately preceding this observation are very illuminating. The hour begins with the Rat Man's angry thoughts at an older sister (Constanze). These lead directly to fantasies of the rat torture (his 'great obsessive fear') being applied to her and then to himself. Associations and interpretations by Freud connect these fantasies with anal-pleasurable feelings associated with itching in the anus and enemas received as a child and then 'the greatest fright of his life': he was playing with a stuffed bird when he felt its wings move and was terrified it had come to life. Freud connects this with the death of the patient's other older sister (Katherine) which occurred when he was about four or five. Freud then states, 'I gave another interpretation of it, (the dead) bird seemingly come to life) namely as an erection caused by the action of his hands. I traced the connection with death from his having been threatened with death at a prehistoric period if he touched himself and brought about an erection of his penis, and suggested that he attributed his sister's death to masturbating' (p. 309).

This passage then leads to the material on sexual looking in place of touching. Other material in the original notes indicates that the patient engaged in sexual play with his sisters, including Katherine who died. Thus, it seems likely that sexual touching came to acquire a very special significance for the Rat Man: he was told that is he 'touched himself' he would die (and/or that his penis would be cut off): he then engaged in sexual touching with his sisters, and Katherine did die – giving a terrifying reality to the threats in his young mind. As an adolescent and adult, the arousal of sexual feelings, especially when mixed with anger toward women, rearoused this terrible fear. 'Looking' evolved as a compromise by which he obtained some pleasure while avoiding what he was convinced, unconsciously, would lead to *death*.

This explanation seems Freudian enough and one might ask why I go into such detail about it. I do so to contrast it with the 'sexual theory of neurosis,' as in the passage already quoted from the 'Three Essays,' which implies that looking is always, or routinely, motivated by sexual energy or libido. I think this example from the Rat Man case shows that it takes a very special set of circumstances – growing up in a family/society which makes terrible threats to children about their sexual–sensual play and the actual death of a sibling involved in such play – to create the intense unconscious conflicts around sexual arousal, feeling, touching and the subsequent compromise substitution of looking for touching.

THE METAPSYCHOLOGY AS A NEUROTIC SYMPTOM

To sum up the discussion so far: we have seen how Freud's thought moved off from the early cases in 'The Studies' in several directions. The early hypotheses implicated traumatic experiences and a number of affective or emotional states which became disturbed or blocked and that were connected with anxiety and a variety of neurotic symptoms. These affects and states included sexuality, anger, fear, death, grief, and others. In addition, these early works present the essential psychoanalytic conception of the symbolic transformation of experience. This model is central to the theory of neurosis as an expression of unconscious conflicts, and is elaborated in the books and papers dealing with dreams, jokes, the psychopathology of everyday life, sexual perversions, and related topics.

While all these ideas were kept alive in Freud's writings in various ways, the causal theory or metapsychology that he pursued in his subsequent works tended to reduce these various phenomena to positions of secondary importance, and to elevate sexuality to the primary motive. In addition, sexuality as a concrete activity observed in the clinical cases was conflated in the metapsychology with much more general ideas concerning the discharge of energy. The reductive, neuropsychological model of 'The Project,' with all its mechanistic, dualistic assumptions, was brought back into the psychological theory in a new guise: it makes its appearance as the model of the mind in Chapter 7 of 'The Interpretation of Dreams,' and appears thereafter in the language of libidinal energy, cathexis, pleasure as the discharge of energy, and related ideas. The metapsychology thus brings together two powerful, conventional trends: the belief that theory should have a physicalist-mechanistic form and the belief that sexuality is basically a harmful activity. What happened thereafter is somewhat difficult to follow because these two trends are confounded. Here is how it worked, as I see it: Freud's early views on the causal role of sexuality in the neuroses were based on the conventional antisex ideas of his time. The neuropsychological model of the mind, taken from other sources, contained the idea of energy buildup and discharge. In all versions of the metapsychology – from 'The Project' and 'The Interpretation of Dreams' on – *pain* is defined as the buildup of energy and *pleasure* is equated with energy discharge. These two conceptual schemes are loosely connected together with 'sexual discharge' - presumably ejaculation and/or orgasm - as the semantic link. The conventional idea that most sexual pleasure - too much, too little, masturbation - is harmful appears in the metapsychology as the seemingly abstract idea of the accumulation of energy: the disruptive effects of excess libido, the id as a 'seething cauldron,' the pleasure principle leading to death, and related notions. Since these more abstract appearing ideas were disconnected from their early roots, they did not change as Freud, as a result of insights gained in his clinical work, came to see sexuality quite differently. In this respect, *the metapsychology is like a neurotic symptom, the encapsulated nature of its infantile core is not modified by later reality testing*.

We now know that both as a neuropsychology *and* a theory of sexuality, the metapsychology is a failure. [4] Yet, it has lingered on because it is linked with these two important aspects of the conventional world view. It has remained, in other words, because it is politically safe: it gives the appearance of tying psychoanalysis to science, on the one hand, and dissociating it from any hint of sexual libertinism, on the other. Both of these are mistaken aims, the first for the reasons I elaborated in the preceding chapter, and the second because it runs counter to what psychoanalysis should really be about: the liberation of the individual from the crippling anxiety and guilt of the past.

FREUD'S FLUID STYLE

Conventional and critical perspectives are interwoven throughout much of Freud's work. Indeed, it was not uncommon for him to write from both points of view in the same paper; and this was as true of theoretical works as it was of case material. How was he able to keep these contradictory perspectives in coexistence for so long? One way was by ignoring inconsistencies and contradictions - in this he illustrates Emerson's epigram that 'a foolish consistency is the hobgoblin of little minds.' He did this with a very unique style, a style that enabled him to seem scientific when writing about human affairs and human when constructing physicalistic theory. It is characteristic of the style that, on the one hand, he populates the metapsychology with all sorts of personalized, emotional, intentional imagery while on the other, the accounts of real persons in action - the case studies and clinical examples - are encumbered with mechanistic terminology and explanations. An examination of this stylistic interweaving of perspectives will also reveal the way the conventional views regarding sexuality were carried forward in disguised form.

Here is an example, taken from Chapter 7 of 'The Interpretation of Dreams':

It may happen that the sleeping ego takes a still large share in the constructing of the dream, that it reacts to the satis-

fying of the repressed wish with violent indignation and itself
puts an end to the dream with an outburst of anxiety
(p. 55).
We see how a purportedly mechanistic model is animated, is
brought to life, with human imagery. This same fluid blending
of assumptions and images is characteristic of most of Freud's
theoretical work. [5]

Two of the key metapsychological papers are 'On Narcissism:
An Introduction' (1914) and 'Institute and their Vicissitudes'
(1915a). In both of these, Freud begins by outlining a conception of instinct in terms of 'stimuli,' 'reflexes,' 'energy,' and
'discharge,' while, at the same time, describing these instincts
in a language that animates and humanizes them. Thus, in the
1915 paper, the 'nervous system' has the 'task . . . of mastering
stimuli' (p. 120); instincts 'exert pressure' and have 'aims' which
may be 'passive' or 'active' (p. 122); and these 'aims' are directed
to 'objects' which may be other persons or parts of one's own
body (p. 123). In the 1914 paper he speaks of 'an indifferent
psychical energy which only becomes libido through the act of
cathecting an object' (p. 78). These examples may be taken as
descriptions of a mechanical system, but the style – the words
and images – leave them open to an anthropomorphic interpretation
as well. For it is we humans who have 'tasks' to be 'mastered,'
whose lives are filled with 'aims' and 'purposes,' who are sometimes 'active' and at other times 'passive,' and who seek satisfaction in others ('objects') and our own bodies. And surely only
living beings can feel 'indifferent'!

Freud's style permits him to keep the two perspectives in a
state of uneasy coexistence. But it served another purpose as
well, for the conventional view of a menacing sexual instinct is
perpetuated in these papers albeit disguised as metapsychological
theory. In 'Instincts and their Vicissitudes' Freud speaks of
'stimuli' from the 'outer world' which impinge on 'living tissue'
which acts to 'discharge' such stimulation. This describes the
relationship between organism and reality. 'Instincts' are also
'stimuli,' but they have a different origin: instincts are 'stimuli
to the mind.' That is, Freud makes the distinction between
stimuli which arise outside the organism (reality) and those which
arise within, equating instincts with this second group. Since
they arise within us, we cannot escape them. Instinct

> Never operates as a force giving a *momentary* impact but
> always as a *constant* one. Moreover since it impinges not
> from without but from within the organism, no flight can
> avail against it (S.E., vol. 14, p. 118).

And later:

> It (the organism) will be aware of stimuli which can be avoided
> by muscular action (flight); these it ascribes to an external
> world. On the other hand, it will also be aware of stimuli
> against which such action is of no avail and whose character
> of constant pressure persists in spite of it; these stimuli are
> the sign of an internal world, the evidence of instinctual needs
> (p. 119).

A bit further, Freud restates the basic tendency of the organism:
> The nervous system is an apparatus which has the function
> of getting rid of the stimuli that reach it, or of reducing them
> to the lowest possible level; or which, if it were feasible, would
> maintain itself in an altogether unstimulated condition (p. 120).

These quotations point up an essential underlying assumption
of the metapsychology: nature, and our own nature, are both
against us. 'Reality' is pictured as 'stimuli' which irritate the
organism, who attempts to flee from it. Nothing is said about
stimuli of an inherent attractiveness that the organism is drawn
towards. Instinct is the inner 'reality' and it, too, is an irritant
from which one seeks escape. But since it is 'inside,' escape is
impossible. Pleasure consists in the absence of stimulation.

The conception of instinct-sexuality, brought out in these
quotations, is revealing in a number of ways. Many of the assumptions of the conventional world view are operative: the passive-
reactive organism pushed and pulled by physical forces and
energies, and the tendency to view life in dualistic or 'split'
terms: and environment which impinges on an organism that is
separate from it, a body which impinges on an independently
existing mind. And, finally, there is the assumption of the
antagonistic nature of instincts themselves. Instinct is a 'force'
that 'impinges . . . no flight can avail against it.' Thus instinct,
even more than reality, is an enemy.

Our instincts – and sex is the main referent here – are
against us; they disturb our peaceful-pleasurable state and we
strive to escape them. They arise from our bodies as 'stimuli
upon the mind' – irritants – and thus our bodies, too, are against
us. Such 'instinctual force' is likened to an external reality
which, while not as persistently irritating, is still a potential
disrupter of our happiness. Thus, the embattled organism is
besieged by hostile forces from within his own body and from the
outside world; one might almost call this a paranoid version of
human nature. Lest the reader think I am exaggerating Freud's
view, simply think of the way the relationships between instinct,
person and environment are presented in such later works as
'The Ego and the Id' (1923). What is earlier termed instinct becomes 'the id,' the 'seething cauldron' of impulses ever threatening to erupt. And what is here 'the organism' is later 'the ego,'
steering its precarious way between id-instinct, the moral
commands of the superego, and a threatening reality. Here is
how Freud puts it in 'The New Introductory Lectures' of 1933:
> The poor ego has things even worse: it serves three severe
> masters and does what it can to bring their claims and demands
> into harmony with one another. These claims are always
> divergent and often seem incompatible. No wonder that the ego
> so often fails in its task. Its three tyrannical masters are the
> external world, the superego and the id. . . . It feels hemmed
> in on three sides, threatened by three kinds of dangers, to
> which, if it is hard pressed, it reacts by generating anxiety
> (p. 77).

Again, it is worth stressing that another image is simultaneously alive in Freud, one that relates instinct and sexuality
to eros or love, to the great binding forces of human social life.
Where the first view sees sexuality in terms of split-up acts -
intercourse, masturbation, perversions - that discharge energy
and give pleasure to individuals who are termed 'objects,' the
second speaks of interactions between whole persons who love,
hate, give pleasure - sexual and in other forms - as well as
punish, cause to feel guilty, act inhumane, loving, perverted,
and a thousand other ways, in the course of their lives together.
This second trend is present even in the 'Narcissism' and
'Instincts' papers. In both essays, the metapsychological formulations appear in the beginning and, in both, homage is paid to
physiological reductionism; that is, there are attempts to link
'libido' with the biological functions of sexuality and the hope
is expressed that some day all will be explained in 'scientific'
terms. But as the essays progress, these trends fade and the
main focus of Freud's interest becomes clear: 'On Narcissism' is
a discussion of the course of human love, and particularly of
the complex interplay between love of self and love of others.
It contains much more as well: ideas about schizophrenia, the
origins of conscience and the development of male and female
identity - all topics that in no way can be reduced to physiological mechanisms or energies. 'Instincts and their Vicissitudes'
deals with closely related themes and turns, in its later sections,
to a discussion of the course of love and hate, and the *ambivalence* characteristic of intense human relationships. If the early
version of instinct suggested that a 'scientific' metapsychology,
if taken literally, was of little use to Freud's central concerns,
the later sections of these papers make clear what these concerns
are. And they make clear, as well, that *the metapsychological
language is almost wholly metaphorical, it is a way of describing
the inner or symbolic representations of human emotions and
relationships*.

WHY THE AMBIVALENCE REMAINED UNRESOLVED

The examples just reviewed illustrate how Freud, with his
particular style, maintained the two world views in an uneasy
coexistence. It was important to him to retain his connection
with the past - with reason, science, objectivity and conventional society - as he opened up the new reality of the unconscious. He did so for several reasons. His scientific education
created a strong predisposition in favor of theory phrased in
a language of forces, objects, and energies. In addition, this
commitment to a particular version of science coincided with his
personal ambitions. A good scientific theory was one that
brought diverse phenomena together in a simple or elegant
explanatory framework. The more observations that could be
accounted for by a small number of principles, the more 'power-

ful' the principles appeared to be. In this sense, Freud was
looking for the psychological laws of gravity, a kind of theory
building that fit well with his ambitions, for we know by his own
account how disappointed he was at not receiving recognition
for his early work with cocaine, or how he envisioned a plaque
being erected to commemorate his discovery of the meaning of
dreams. In 'The Studies' and other early papers we see him
struggling with the prevalent diagnostic terminology: 'hysteria,'
'neurasthenia,' 'psychasthenia,' 'obsessional neurosis,' 'actual
neuroses.' What could all these conditions have in common? He
searches for a principle that will provide a unifying explanation
and finally discovers, or invents, it: *sexuality*. Thus, his discovery of the role of sexuality in the neuroses, and his attempt
to frame it as a single wide-sweeping causal force, linked up
with conventional science through the metapsychology, is his
bid to become the *Newton of the mind*.

Freud's commitment to science and his personal ambition
played their roles in the creation of a theory built around
sexuality as a single, quasi-physical force. And they account,
as well, for the retention of this theory long after it could have
been abandoned in the face of new argument and clinical evidence.
But these were not the major reasons for the persistence of this
position. They capture part of the truth, they point up the role
of the male-heroic in Freud, the scientist and man of reason, the
ambitious male whose courage took him into realms where others
feared to venture. But there was a larger reason for the persistence of the conventional view of sexuality, one more complex
and difficult to describe. It was this: using the new method of
psychoanalysis, Freud found himself confronted with the
horrible underside of modern society: the exploitation of women;
the corruption of love and pleasure; the mistreatment of children
in the most respectable of families; death, loss and separations,
so badly mourned, so incompletely dealt with; and madness –
insanity itself – with its terrifying fears and painful consequences.
The neurotics he worked with were, in this sense, the victims of
civilized progress, their unconscious conflicts, and his own as
he came to see in his self-analysis, contained the symbolic record
of their victimization. The disturbance in their sexuality –
especially when this referred to relationships of love, affection
and sensual gratification rather than the discharge of libidinal
energy – was certainly a painful side of their civilized lives, but
it was by no means the whole story.

Now when one confronts a truth like this, a truth that most
members of respectable society have a stake in denying, one
can adopt a revolutionary stance and show others the realities
they would rather not see, or one can go along with the pre-
vailing rationalizations. Freud does both. On the one hand, he
confronts his society with its own denied secrets and develops
a method which provides access to the disguised, unconcious
side of life. And he formulates a critical theory about this
secret realm: it is driven by sexuality – a sexuality in which love

has been corrupted by anxiety and painful symptoms. But he also constructs a scientific-appearing theory - the metapsychology - that turns away from painful human experience, from socially induced conflict and, in effect, blames all on the sexual instinct itself. If there are conflicts in the unconscious, if neurotics suffer disturbance in their sexual lives, it is because libido is an antisocial, narcissistic, disruptive force. In this second view, sexuality becomes a scapegoat, just as women, children, and the feminine, soft and loving side of men were scapegoats.

THREE WOMEN: ANNA O., KATHARINA AND DORA

In much of the discussion so far, I have implied that the conventional view of sexuality is bound up with similar prejudicial views of women and the wider set of qualities deemed feminine: love, maternity, softness, emotionality. Freud's treatment of these qualities reveals the same mixture of perspectives as his treatment of sexuality; psychoanalysis is both forerunner of the liberation of women - and the feminine side of men - and tied to the conventional emphasis on rigid sex-role boundaries. The unfinished journey in this sphere helps explain the very divergent reaction of contemporary feminist writers to Freud: some see him as ally and others as enemy.[6] The mixed treatment of women and femininity is best examined in three of Freud's cases, to which we now turn.

Anna O. is the first of the five 'hysterics' - all were women - discussed in 'The Studies.' Her initial breakdown arose out of the long vigil she kept by the bedside of her dying father. She collapsed with a great variety of symptoms: she would be in and out of different states of consciousness, slept or kept to her bed during the day and was awake most of the night, developed various somatic complaints - paralyses and partial paralyses, disturbances of vision and hearing, loss of appetite and/or peculiar eating habits, a severe 'nervous cough' - and had terrifying hallucinations of death's heads and skeletons. There was much anger and symbolic rebellion in her 'sickness,' much fear, anxiety, guilt and self-punishment, including strong suicidal impulses, and much depression. She was a person with other qualities as well:

> This girl, who was bubbling over with intellectual vitality, led an extremely monotonous existence in her puritanically-minded family. She embellished her life in a manner which probably influenced her decisively in the direction of her illness, by indulging in systematic day-dreaming, which she described as her 'private theatre' (p. 22).

How much is contained in this brief description. Breuer and Freud focus on the habitual use of fantasy in the prebreakdown period as a clue to understanding the form her illness took. Their discussion moves on to detail her symptoms and the complicated course of her illness which began during the period when she devoted her full energy to nursing her dying father. But what about the 'monotonous existence' and the 'puritanically-minded' family? We know that women at this time, no matter how energetic and intelligent, had little opportunity to be other than wives, mothers and servants to men. Anna was extremely talented; during her illness she expressed herself, apparently with great competence, in four different languages; Breuer describes her as 'markedly intelligent, with an astonishingly quick grasp of things and penetrating intuition.' Anna literally worked herself into a state of mental collapse as she cared for the father of whom she was 'passionately fond,' and whom she no doubt secretly resented. Her family seemed to think it quite acceptable that an intelligent and attractive young woman should 'love her father' even when this trapped her in a romantic relationship without possibility of mature fulfillment; it kept her in a position of rivalry with her mother and blocked relationships with other men. And beyond this, the family seemed unaware of what was happening to her, nor did they try to prevent her from driving herself into a state of insanity.

All of this is there to be seen in the case of Anna O., the complex way in which her neurosis reflected her exploitation within a father-dominated family. But, although Freud and Breuer present us with the material to view Anna in this way, this is not what they themselves focus on. Their emphasis - and this is very clear in Freud's final chapter - is on the blocked sexuality per se. This was a central feature of Anna's conflicts to be sure, but it can only be understood within the larger con- text of patriarchy and the limited opportunities open to women, and her particular exploitation as a woman within her family. [7]

The second case to be considered is Katharina, a young woman whom Freud encountered while he was on vacation in the mountains. It is the briefest of the cases reported in 'The Studies.' She approached Freud, knowing he was a doctor, and described her complaints: shortness of breath, pains in the head, a crushing feeling in her chest, and a frightening image of an angry male face. With his striking powers of observation and intuition, Freud determined that she was suffering from anxiety and hysteria and traced the symptoms to certain traumatic sexual experiences.

In the original version of the case, Katharina is described as living with her 'aunt' and 'uncle.' The symptoms first arose when she accidentally discovered the uncle having sexual intercourse with her 'cousin.' She was upset and frightened at the discovery, and anxiety - shortness of breath, hammering in the head - appeared later in the form of her neurotic symptoms. Freud pursued the matter and discovered that the sight of the uncle and cousin was traumatic because it connected to memories of earlier experiences in which the uncle had attempted to force himself on Katharina sexually (she was fourteen years old at the time). Katharina later told her aunt of the attempted seduc- tion, a revelation that led to angry disputes with the uncle and

an eventual divorce. During that time, the uncle was particularly
outraged at her - hence the image of the angry male face that
was part of her symptom picture.

In his discussion of this case, Freud focuses on the connections between the sexual experiences and the symptoms, the
way the girl is unaware of these connections, and how he was
able to bring them to consciousness and provide some relief or
cure. The experiences were traumatic because 'a mere suspicion
of sexual relations calls up the affect of anxiety in virginal
individuals' (p. 134). It is clear from his discussion that he views
the trauma as resulting from the exposure to sex at an immature
age; that is, things would presumably have gone better for
Katharina if she had been appropriately sheltered from the
frightening facts of life.

In a footnote to the case of Katharina, added in 1924, Freud
reveals that the 'aunt' and 'uncle' were, in fact, her mother and
father. He states, 'The girl fell ill, therefore, as a result of
sexual attempts on the part of her own father' (p. 134). We can
add, from the evidence he makes available, that not only did
her father attempt to seduce her on several occasions, and
presumably successfully seduced her sister - the 'cousin' whom
she caught him with - but later turned on her in anger and
attempted to blame her for the breakup of the marriage. In the
light of these factors, one sees it was not her exposure to
sexuality at an immature period that was traumatic, but an
exposure to incestuous, guilt-inducing attempts at seduction by
the father whom she was dependent on, probably loved and
desired, and clearly feared: all at an age when she could not
very well understand these matters and was not in a position to
deal with them, except by developing a neurotic illness. As in
the case of Anna O., Freud's glimpse into the world of family
relationships, as revealed in Katharina's unconscious, shows the
complex effects of sexual victimization in a male-dominated society.

Freud's handling of the case of Katharina reveals his vacilla-
tion between two different views of sexuality. On the one hand,
he exposes the secret family conflicts, feeling compelled to tell
the truth about Katharina's seduction by her father in a footnote added almost thirty years after the original publication of
the case. Yet, on the other hand, his theoretical explanation
continues to trace the neurotic symptoms to the evils of sexuality
per se: that it was the mere exposure to sex - the primal scene -
that traumatized the 'virginal' Katharina.

Dora is Freud's longest case study of a woman. He wrote it in
1901 but delayed publication for five years. The case is a complicated one and I will only comment on it briefly to illustrate
the issues under consideration. (The interested reader should
see the original, S.E., vol. 7, and the cogent discussions of
Erikson, 1964, pp. 166-74; Lewin, 1973; and Marcus, 1974.)

Dora, aged eighteen, a girl 'in the first bloom of youth of
intelligent and engaging looks,' is brought to Freud by her
father. She enters treatment against her will: 'it was only her

father's authority which induced her to come to me at all,' says
Freud. She suffers from migraine headaches, a nervous cough
that sometimes leads to loss of voice, and other somatic manifestations. She is also - like all the cases in 'The Studies,' by the
way - chronically depressed. Along with these symptoms there
is a good deal of hostility directed at both her mother and father.
She is, in broad terms, an extremely angry and unhappy young
woman who can find no meaningful direction to her life and who is
fast becoming a chronic sufferer, a symptom-ridden neurotic. As
in his discussion of the cases in 'The Studies,' Freud's main
purpose is to unravel the meaning of Dora's symptoms in relation
to her life experiences. The case is also an extension of 'The
Interpretation of Dreams' and was written to show the connection
between dreams and 'hysteria.' But it contains a great deal
more as well.

Here is a brief outline of Freud's analysis. The father is
wealthy and the dominant figure in the family. Dora, earlier in
her life, loved and idealized him. The mother is described as
suffering from 'housewife's psychosis'; she is a compulsive
drudge, unimaginative and, presumably, sexually unresponsive
to her husband. Dora apparently shares her father's scornful
attitude toward the mother. The family is involved in a complicated
way with another family identified as the 'K's.' Frau K nursed
the father during a protracted illness and, as becomes clear,
they have maintained a sexual liaison for some years. Dora, at
an earlier period, was close with the K's, had intimate conversa-
tions with Frau K, helped care for their young children, and
spent much time with Herr K as well.

The immediate source of her neurotic symptoms, as Freud
discovers in the analysis, are two sexual advances made to Dora
by Herr K. The first occurs when she is fourteen: he grabs her
and kisses her on the mouth, to which she responds with 'a
violent feeling of disgust.' When she is sixteen he makes a
'proposal' when they are out walking in the Alps and she slaps
his face and hurries away. While she had kept the first incident
secret, she tells her parents of the second and is later enraged
at her father's tendency to make light of it and accept Herr K's
version of the event. Freud traces certain of her specific
symptoms to the arousal of conflicted sexual feelings by these
events and, behind them, to what he takes as love for Frau K.

Two lines of explanation are at work in the Dora case. When
Freud comes to explain *why* the arousal of sexual feelings should
produce anxiety, disgust and neurotic symptoms, he primarily
depends on the conventional view: libido or sex is itself the
culprit. Along this line there is much speculation and tracing of
current material to Dora's early history of bed-wetting, masturbation and other forms of infantile sexuality. Typical are his comments on the case in a letter to Fliess in which he refers to

> Solutions of hysterical symptoms and considerations on the
> sexual-organic basis of the whole condition. . . . The case
> is a hysteria with *tussis nervosa* and aphonia, which can be

traced back to the characteristics of a thumb-sucker; and
the principal part in the conflicting mental processes is
played by the opposition between an attraction towards men
and one towards women (S.E., vol. 7, p. 4).

In other words, this line of explanation attributes the cause of
the neurosis to sexual forces within Dora. Either she did not
sufficiently renounce her search for infantile sexual pleasure,
or else she has too much homosexual libido. Consistent with this
focus on the role of her sexual instincts, Freud assumes that
Dora must be sexually aroused by Herr K's overtures for he is,
after all, an attractive male.

The other line of explanation is not formulated explicitly by
Freud, but is implied by much of the evidence that he, with his
characteristic honesty, includes in the case. From this second
point of view, the arousal of sexual feelings in Dora by Herr K's
attention is, from the outset, confounded with the conflicting
loyalties and betrayals in which all the parties are involved.
Frau K is interested in the father, uses Dora as a stepping-stone
to get close to him, and then casts her aside once the liaison is
established. The father, in effect, is handing his daughter over
to Herr K as payment for his affair with Frau K. The unspoken
agreement seems to be, 'You ignore what I am doing with your
wife and I will ignore what you do with my daughter. Thus we
[men] can all obtain the sexual gratification we desire.' And all
the parties lie, cover-up and mystify. Freud himself notes:

> It was possible for Herr K to send Dora flowers every day for
> a whole year while he was in the neighborhood, to take every
> opportunity of giving her valuable presents, and to spend
> all his spare time in her company, without her parents noticing
> anything in his behavior that was characteristic of love-
> making (Ibid., p. 35).

In other passages, Freud reveals that he knows the father
to be a man who lies in pursuit of his own interests. Marcus
sums it up this way:

> In some sense everyone was conspiring to conceal what was
> going on; and in some yet further sense everyone was con-
> spiring to deny that anything was going on at all. What we
> have here, on one of its sides, is a classical Victorian domestic
> drama, that is at the same time a sexual and emotional can of
> worms (Marcus, 1974, p. 15).

'Victorian domestic drama' sounds a bit charming; what is
described is the way a family pattern of deceit and mystification
can drive certain victimized members insane. It is precisely when
Dora insists on telling the truth that her father takes her to
Freud so that he may 'bring her to reason.' As Marcus per-
ceptively notes:

> The three adults to whom she was closest, whom she loved
> the most in the world, were apparently conspiring - separately,
> in tandem, or in concert - to deny her the reality of her
> experience. They were conspiring to deny Dora her reality
> and reality itself. This betrayal touched upon matters that

might easily unhinge the mind of a young person; for the three adults were not betraying Dora's love and trust alone; they were betraying the structure of the actual world (Ibid., p. 17).

In addition to these issues of trust, betrayal and distortion of reality there were serious problems in her attempts at identification as a woman. Her mother was cast aside as a model as Dora attempted to move into her father's orbit. But there, her closeness with Frau K turned out to be a sham and, in a more general way, she came to sense – and express through her moods and symptoms – the way she was being used. It must not have seemed possible to her in that particular family-social network to be a woman without being either a victim or a beaten-down slave like her mother. As Erikson notes in his discussion of her identity struggles,

The specific social and cultural conditions of her place and time, however, determined her milieu's confusing role demands. As a *woman*, Dora did not have a chance (Erikson, 1964, p. 172).

While Dora both suffers and receives some gratification from the family intrigues, in the end she is, like Anna O., and Katharina, the female victim of a society that gave men much more freedom and power to pursue their interests than women. The men do not escape the harmful effects of this unfair social system – Dora's father persistently uses his various 'illnesses' to legitimize his need for love, sexual attention and care. The essence of Dora's dealings with Freud, as he later realizes, is to seek revenge on him as a representative of all the other men – her father, Herr K – who have used and abused her. But the revenge contains a self-damaging side, for while a victim, she has incorporated the assumptions and mystifications of her family-society into herself and so is caught in their web. Her neurosis, her depression, her painful symptoms, her unquenchable need for revenge: all reveal the symbolic version of the social conflicts that she has incorporated. [8]

In sum, the Dora case shows the continued coexistence of the two perspectives in Freud. Theoretically, he explains her illness in terms consistent with the conventional view of the destructive power of sexuality: she is a 'characteristic thumb-sucker,' a 'hysteric' who feels disgust at the sexual overtures of a man who seems, to Freud, to be an attractive suitor. Yet he includes all the other material which implicates the complex social network that makes this sexual seduction disgusting to the victimized young girl. For reasons that no one is sure of, he delayed publishing the case for five years. Perhaps this resulted from the unresolved tension between these two forms of explanation. While in the final passages he comes to recognize the transference reactions – the way in which Dora is taking out her revenge on him – he is still uncertain about 'what a woman wants.'

The case of Dora illustrates that, in a certain sense, both the sexual seduction and the sexual wish theory are true, if these

are encompassed in the larger theory of the symbolic transformation of experience. For while Freud did not uncover any
sexual trauma from early childhood we can see that Dora's
father was screwing her - as slang would put it - in several
ways, including an attempted seduction by his emissary, Herr K.
In a larger symbolic sense, she, her mother, Frau K, and all the
Annas and Katharinas, the governesses, nurses and servant
girls, the housewives and mistresses, were being screwed by the
male-centered society, as well as by their actual fathers, hus-
bands, and masters. And men, too, were victims of this one-
sided culture, their own femininity and maternal feelings
suppressed, their own love and sexuality compromised by guilt
and conflict. It is the symbolic record of all this that Freud
discovered in the unconscious and, again, we see how he took
both a conservative and a radical stance in relation to his discovery. In the neurotic suffering of his patients he sees the
price that is paid for the success, the progress, and the power
of the modern state and, after revealing much of this he draws
back and, in the metapsychology, in the primal scene hypothesis,
and in other views of the sexual instinct, embraces his society's
version: it is the fault of sex itself, of libido.

And yet, and yet. . . . By continuing to do psychoanalysis,
by continuing to listen to his patients, by subtlety of style and
the interweaving of subthemes, and by his ultimate honesty he
kept open a whole new way of seeing these same issues.

5 BISEXUALITY, AUTONOMY AND AUTHORITY: the case of Schreber

The biological difference between male and female is used as an organizing principle in all known human societies. Children are defined as boys and girls at birth and raised in ways that prepare them for their culturally appropriate roles as men and women. One's core sense of masculinity or femininity is acquired early: it is a basic aspect of identity, of who and what one is. There are universal differences between the sexes: women bear children, nurse them and engage in related maternal activities; boys are predisposed to aggressive play which connects, in various ways, to such activities as hunting (primarily a male province in most primitive societies). [1] Yet, while all societies are divided into male-female groups, and while there are universal sex differences, the range of cultural variation in the definition of these differences is quite wide. Of special importance is the rigidity with which different societies enforce sex-role behavior and the concomitant anxiety aroused by the many possible variations in such behavior. To take an example that should be familiar, many middle-class and professional American fathers today participate in the care of their infants, change diapers or get up in the middle of the night to give the baby a bottle. Such behavior would have been unthinkable to a comparable European father in the last century: it would have been an affront to his status and position and felt as inappropriate to his identity as a male. The bounds of appropriate sex-role behavior have loosened somewhat in this area; it is more permissible for men to act maternally.

Western society of the past few centuries has been characterized by relatively rigid sex-role boundaries. The specific cultural definitions of masculinity and femininity have often been taken as God-given universals or as biologically fixed attributes. When we look at the European society of Freud's day, we encounter the well-known Victorian stereotypes: men were supposed to be manly, decisive, in control of their emotions, hard, aggressive; women chaste, pure, retiring, receptive, passive. The actual definition and living of these roles was more complicated than these stereotypes suggest, of course, yet they are easily seen examples of that large exaggeration of the differences between the sexes so characteristic of nineteenth-century Europe. And this exaggeration, in turn, went along with a rigid segregation of the qualities felt to be associated with one sex or the other. Men were to be men and women women; the appearance of 'feminine' characteristics in males, or of 'masculinity' in females, were sources of great anxiety. Real people were not pure sexual types, of course, any more than they are today. There was every gradation, including active-aggressive women and passive-retiring men, not to mention the more striking examples of sex-role 'deviance': overt homosexuality of all sorts or the variety of sexual perversions that displayed a mixture of male and female sexual qualities. But, while one could observe many examples that contradicted the ideal of sex-role purity, these instances were viewed as abnormalities, as signs of immorality, degeneracy and sickness. The situation was directly analogous to that of infantile sexuality, where the cultural ideal of 'innocent' childhood was everywhere contradicted by the real sexual activities of children. Like violations of sex-role boundaries, the sexual acts of children were viewed as immoral, perverse and due to the eruption of dangerous instinct. And, just as Freud's theory of infantile sexuality played its part in the liberation of childhood from oppressive sexual taboos and restrictions, so his theory of universal *bisexuality* played its part in the transformation of what it meant to be male or female.

FREUD'S VIEWS ON BISEXUALITY

The theory of infantile sexuality was a major challenge to the conventional view which separated childhood from the sexual world of adults. Freud demonstrated that, far from appearing suddenly at puberty, sexuality was present from the beginning of life, though in forms quite different from its later manifestations. In a closely related way, the theory of bisexuality breaks down the rigid boundary between masculinity and feminity. It shows how we are each a mixture of so-called masculine and feminine qualities - qualities that we acquire from our early family relationships, and which develop over the course of our lives. Finally, and again like the broader theory of sexuality, Freud's views on bisexuality contain a mixture of conventional assumptions and critical insights, never completely sorted out in his own work.

Freud's first hypotheses concerning bisexuality were taken from the work of his friend Wilhelm Fliess. The essence of these early ideas was fairly simple: one can find traces of the biological characteristics of each sex in the other - truncated secondary sexual characteristics such as nipples on men or the clitoris, which Freud believed was a miniature penis, in women or, as we now know, both male and female hormones in each sex - and these are indices of biological bisexuality. Since the biological was assumed to be 'the basis' for the psychological, there must be a corresponding psychological bisexuality. Freud's commitment to this version of bisexuality did not last very long. By 1905, in the first of the 'Three Essays on the Theory of Sexuality,' he argues that physical or biological bisexuality does not explain very much about the wide range of sexual identity problems - inversions and perversions - that one can observe. He suggests another course, linking masculinity-femininity with activity-passivity. Activity-passivity is also related to sadism-masochism: Freud groups together two opposed sets of psychological-behavioral characteristics: masculinity-activity-sadism and femininity-passivity-masochism. Sometimes he writes as if the connection between these characteristics is problematic. For instance in a footnote added to the 'Three Essays' in 1915, he states:

> In human beings, pure masculinity or femininity is not to be found either in a psychological or a biological sense. Every individual on the contrary displays a mixture of the character traits belonging to his own and to the opposite sex; and he shows a combination of activity and passivity whether or not these last character traits tally with his biological ones (S.E., vol. 7, p. 220).

He makes a similar point in a long footnote to 'Civilization and its Discontents' (S.E., vol. 21, pp. 105-6). But, at other times, he writes as if the connections are fixed: female sexuality is always passive and masochistic, male sexuality active and sadistic. It is never made entirely clear why male and female sexuality should always take these forms. Can one not enjoy passive sexual pleasure that is not connected to masochism, to pain and suffering? Is it not possible for both men and women to be active sexually in loving rather than sadistic ways? Let me be clear: Freud's grouping of these characteristics was based on important observations; he saw many instances of passive-masochistic sexuality in women, for example. What is never made clear in his own writings was whether such links were universal, 'biological' and inevitably tied to one's sex or were a function of one's particular social-life experience. In sum: the idea that everyone is a mixture of male and female qualities was a revolutionary and liberating insight in a society committed to sexual purity and a rigid separation of the sexes, a society that was quite threatened by any mixing or blurring of sex roles. The description of the many forms of sexual suffering in masochism and sadism and their symbolic elaboration was similarly insightful. But the theory also contains remnants of the past: the connection with biology was never clearly worked through, which gave an aura of inevitability to the particular social-historical definitions of masculinity and femininity. Sexual pleasure remained under a cloud of suspicion and passive or 'feminine' longings were seen as dangerous inner temptations in men (as we will see shortly in Freud's analysis of Schreber).

Yet while the theory of bisexuality was never completely worked through, Freud's ideas on the formation of sexual identity, developed in another context, provide the components for a coherent, critical theory of psychological-bisexual conflict. In 'The Ego and the Id' of 1923, he describes the way in which the ego and the superego develop from identifications with the parents during the Oedipus complex. He specifically notes the fourfold process in which the male or female child finds him/herself in relations of love and rivalry with both the mother and father at different times and to different degrees. Thus, in addition to the well-known 'positive Oedipus complex,' in which the boy takes his mother as a love object, feels his father as a rival and, eventually, identifies with the father's masculinity, the boy also takes his father as a love object – feels himself in a passive-feminine relation to him – with his mother as a rival. Without going into the details of this process we may, for our present purposes, extract the underlying model. This is a model that traces sexual identity – one's sense of maleness or femaleness – to identifications with the important emotional figures of childhood. Since we are raised in a world filled with crucial male and female figures (fathers and mothers, or their substitutes, male and female siblings), our egos – our personalities or selves – develop from these male and female identifications. The child identifies with its father or mother, or with different aspects of each, depending on his or her own inclinations and talents and the specific nature of the emotional relationships with the parents.[2]

The essential point to take from this model is that bisexuality is largely the result of these identifications. One's inner maleness and femaleness, the way qualities associated with each sex – competitiveness, passivity, achievement – are experienced, as well as conflicts between them, are the results of our childhood experiences with males and females, and the way we have incorporated these experiences into ourselves. Sexual identity and bisexuality are influenced as well by our contact with the social definition and treatment of masculine and feminine qualities. From our contact with parents, siblings and the other emotional figures of childhood, we acquire our characteristic orientation toward assertiveness and submission; we learn how to be loving, caring and maternal, as well as aggressive and competitive; we play at a variety of incipient roles and actions, both male and female. And we learn which of these roles and actions are valued by society and which are not. It is from this kind of social-psychological experience that we acquire the basis of our two sexual sides, as well as the basis for conflict between them. In other words, the conflicts of bisexuality do not arise purely from some constitutional or biological source; rather, they are the reflection within the adult personality of the characteristic sexual conflicts of the males and females with whom one was raised.

The two best known aspects of sexual-identity conflict delineated by Freud are 'penis-envy' in women and 'latent homosexuality' in men. These conflicts were and are there to be observed in many men and women, of course; the point of debate, contested by femininists and others, concerns the biological inevitability of such conflicts. Within a critical theory of sexual identity, the woman's envy of the penis as a symbol of male privilege and 'superiority,' and the man's fear of his feminine qualities, can be seen as examples of bisexual conflict arising from early experiences of identification within families and societies that value and devalue boys and girls in particular ways.

In a larger sense, there are as many versions of inner bisexual
conflict as there are social conflicts between men and women,
as there are attacks on feminine qualities, as there are over-
evaluations of maleness – with all the jealousies, rivalries, envy,
latent anger, sadism, masochism, guilt and fear that accompany
such conflicts. [3]

THE CASE OF SCHREBER

Daniel Paul Screber was a prominant German judge in the late
nineteenth century. He suffered a severe and incapacitating
psychosis in which he believed he was being persecuted by
his doctors, and by God, and that his male body was being
feminized. Schreber eventually recovered and wrote an account
of his experience. This account, published in 1903 as 'Denkwürdigkeiten eines Nervenkranken'[4] ('Memoirs of My Mental
Illness') came to Freud's attention; he used it as the basis for
the psychoanalytic study of Schreber in which he developed his
theory of the causal role of 'latent homosexuality' in paranoia,
one of his major theoretical treatments of the male's fear of his
femininity. Freud's analysis of Schreber is a particularly good
example of the unfinished journey. For, if it is true, as I have
been arguing, that Freud's own theories were developing along
the dimensions male-centered to bisexual, conventional to
critical and rational-objective to intuitive-subjective, Schreber
himself displayed a much more extreme version of these same
developments, He believed his male body was becoming feminized,
that he was engaged in a personal battle with the highest authority,
God, and that all that happened to him was beyond the realm of
science and rationality and could only be understood as a
subjective-revelatory experience. Given these facts, it will be
of the greatest interest to examine Freud's analysis of Schreber:
to note what he sees and what he does not see in the case.
    There are several other features which make Schreber, of
all Freud's cases, an especially interesting candidate for detailed
consideration. There are other sources of information and interpretation, in addition to Freud's, available in this case. The
'Memoirs' themselves give Schreber's own account and interpretation of what happened to him and if, following Freud's lead, we
view them as a meaningful symbolic communication – rather than
as 'delusional' or psychotic nonsense – we may compare Schreber's
own intepretation with Freud's. In addition to the 'Memoirs,'
much additional information has come to light in recent years
concerning Schreber's father, his family and the general system
of values and child training methods in which he grew up (see
Niederland, 1974 and Schatzman, 1973). Since this information
was not available to Freud it allows us to view the case, now,
from a much expanded framework.
    Schreber's father was a leading 'expert' on family life and the
raising of children; he published numerous books on these topics

which were widely read throughout Europe during the second half of the nineteenth century. The values and practices that these books espouse give a detailed picture of such topics as: conceptions of infancy and childhood, male and female roles, sexuality, pleasure, work, discipline, and individual-authority relationships. The father's ideas give a flavor of the world view that shaped the childhoods of both Freud and Schreber. All of this information - the 'Memoirs,' the father's books, and new historical data on childhood and family life in nineteenth-century Europe - gives a more complete picture of Schreber's background than was available to Freud. We can now see more clearly the extent to which his analysis of Schreber remains within the conventional world view and the extent to which it moves to the new psychoanalytic perspective.

Schreber
Daniel Paul Schreber was born in 1842, the third of five children in a prominent family: a number of ancestors on both his mother's and father's side were distinguished scientists, doctors, judges and professors. Schreber's father, whose work we will examine in detail shortly, was a widely known physician, orthopedist, and zealous advocate of exercise and the active life. To this day many city-dwelling Germans tend their Schrebergärten - small plots of land in the country - a practice inspired by the father. Schreber himself had a distinguished early career as a lawyer and judge. He was a doctor of jurisprudence, stood as a candidate for the Reichstag (parliament), and eventually reached the position of presiding judge - of what corresponds in our system to a Court of Appeals - in the city of Dresden.

He suffered his first mental breakdown at the age of forty-two, following his defeat for the Reichstag, a breakdown that was labeled 'severe hypochondriasis' at the time, and that consisted of marked sleep disturbance, difficulty eating and other somatic manifestations. He was hospitalized in the clinic of Dr Paul Theodore Flechsig, one of the leading neuroanatomists of the time, and was discharged after six months, apparently recovered and able to return to work. Nine years later, at the age of fifty-one, Schreber suffered a more severe collapse shortly after his appointment as presiding judge to the high court in Dresden. He spent the next nine years of his life in mental hospitals where he experienced the symptoms of what today would be called a severe paranoid schizophrenic psychosis. He lost the socially accepted sense of reality; was often catatonic or immobile, and at other times violent; refused to eat or bathe and tried to kill himself. He believed that the world had come to an end and that only he was really alive: that the people he saw around him were 'fleetingly improvised men.' At other times he would bellow violently at the sun. He felt that his doctors and attendants interfered with many aspects of his life, made fun of him, and intended to 'unman' him.

Toward the end of this second confinement, the more disruptive elements of his behavior receded and he tried to make sense of what had happened to him. He began by writing notes on scraps of paper and eventually brought these together in his book, 'Memoirs of My Nervous Illness.' He sought his release from the hospital and attempted to publish the book and, after legal battles with the authorities, achieved both of these goals. In the 'Memoirs,' Schreber describes his psychotic experience in detail and formulates a *neuro-psychotheological* theory to explain what had happened to his body, his mind, and his soul. He became convinced that his first psychiatrist, Flechsig, and then God Himself, had been persecuting him by causing all sorts of painful 'miracles' to be visited on his body. The chaotic mass of his psychosis is given order and meaning by Schreber in the explanation formulated in the 'Memoirs.'

Here, in summary form, is his account. His condition was the result, he came to believe, of God's actions having become out of phase with 'the Order of the World.' The human soul is contained in 'nerves' and God is all soul or 'pure nerve.' Ordinarily, human soul-nerves ascend to God after the death of the body, having first to pass through a period of purification and testing. There, they dwell with God in a state of bliss, a state of uninterrupted feelings of voluptuousness and pleasure. God only rarely contacts living beings, for human nerves, especially in a state of excitement, may attract Him so strongly that He will be held fast to them. Unfortunately, this dangerous attraction of God's nerves occurred in Schreber's own case. Something went wrong involving Schreber, Flechsig, God, and 'the Order of Things', such that God's nerves – in the form of 'rays' (his image fuses nerve impulses, rays of the sun, and spermatozoa) – are especially attracted to Schreber's own nerves. This results in the torture-like 'miracles' of Schreber's psychosis. God is stuck in Schreber's body, His rays interefere with Schreber's every movement and function. Almost no part of Schreber's body is free of these miraculous tortures; foul-tasting 'souls' are forced into his stomach; pains are visited on his neck, his back, and his legs; he cannot move freely, nor eat, nor sleep without some form of divine interference. God does not even let him urinate or defecate in peace, always seeing to it that the toilet is occupied when Schreber needs it.

Throughout these descriptions, we see that Schreber's conception of God is curiously ambivalent. On the one hand, he pictures himself as an insignificant and powerless creature in awe of an omniscient and omnipresent Being; yet, on the other, God's actions in relation to him are for the most part trivial, petty and malicious.

Things can only be put right or returned to their proper order if Schreber himself is transformed from a man to a woman. God's rays will then find pleasure – sensations of 'spiritual voluptuousness' – in Schreber's body and a more harmonious state will be restored between God and mankind. Thus, the idea of Schreber's personal sexual transformation flows from the logic

of his theory; it is part of the 'solution' to the problem posed
by his painful psychotic experiences. When he is transformed
into a woman, his personal pain will become pleasure, and the
world at large will be set back on its proper course.

The central imagery used to describe his relations with God
fuses Christian and scientific terms and ideas in a terminology
of 'rays' and 'nerves.' The Christian aspect may strike the
intellectual of today as odd, but we must remember that Schreber,
like many well-educated men of his time, was much more imbued
with religious values than are comparable figures today. The
imagery is not only religious; Schreber incorporates much of the
science that he was familiar with into his picture of rays and
nerves. [5]

As Schreber formulated this explanation for his psychotic
experience, his more violent and tumultuous state passed; he
became, once more, the intelligent, articulate, and polite man
he had been in his days as a judge. He continued to believe in
the divine nature of his revelations, however, and remained
convinced that he was being transformed into a woman. In
addition, he felt his religious experience contained an important
message for mankind. The 'Memoirs' is an evangelistic document;
Schreber expresses a certain urgency about his message which
is a warning to his fellowmen about God's dangerous ways: 'God
was, if I may so express it, quote incapable of dealing with
living men, and was only accustomed to communicate with
corpses' . . . or God's 'more or less absurd ideas, which were
all *contrary* to human nature' ('Memoirs,' p. 127). Additional
details of Schreber's life and ideas will be examined later in the
section that describes his childhood.

Almost all of Schreber's contemporaries considered him insane,
and he spent most of his later years confined in institutions. The
'Memoirs' did not inspire a religion, and the religious and medical
authorities of his time were content to label it the work of a mad-
man. This was not the case with Freud, who published a major
case study in 1911 based on Schreber's 'Memoirs.'

Freud's analysis
Freud is aware that Schreber was insane in almost any sense of
the term, yet his analysis moves well beyond the conception of
insanity held by his psychiatric contemporaries. He treats the
belief system - Schreber's 'delusion' - as a meaningful communication. In this he diverged from descriptive psychiatry by insist-
ing on *analysis* and *understanding* as opposed to pejorative
labeling. Thus, for Freud, the 'Memoirs' are like the manifest
content of a dream which must be decoded, or translated, into
understandable terms. In addition, Freud notes that 'the delusional
formation, which we take to be the pathological product, is in
reality an attempt at recovery, a process of reconstruction' (1911,
p. 71). So the 'Memoirs' are not only meaningful, in Freud's
view, but psychologically reparative.

The idea that the beliefs of a 'psychotic' are meaningful, and that their analysis can lead to an understanding of insanity, is in the revolutionary new spirit of psychoanalysis. But when we examine the specific content of Freud's analysis – and particularly his treatment of paternal authority and sexuality – we encounter the mixture of criticial and conventional values that is by now familiar. Freud begins his analysis of Schreber by bringing to bear a psychoanalytic concept – transference – which is used to decode Schreber's ideas about Flechsig and God. The ideas and feelings that he experienced in relation to his psychiatrist and God are seen as projections of his fantasies, particularly his unconscious, childhood wishes and feelings regarding his father. 'The Patient's struggle with Flechsig became revealed to him as a conflict with God, and we must therefore construe it as an infantile conflict with the father whom he loved; the details of that conflict [of which we know nothing] are what determined the content of the delusion' (p. 55). Already, we see that it is the son's love – shortly to be defined as 'latent homosexual' or passive feminine sexual impulses – that is the underlying disruptive force.

Freud recognizes that he is on speculative ground in his treatment of the father-son relationship since he has no direct evidence concerning Schreber's early life. Nevertheless, he assumes that it is the son's *impulses* and *fantasies* that are at the root of the threat and even guesses:

That what enables Schreber to reconcile himself to his homosexual fantasy, and so made it possible for his illness to terminate in something approximating to a recovery, may have been the fact that his father-complex was in the main positively toned and that in real life the later years of his relationship with an excellent father had probably been unclouded (p. 78).

At another point, he notes:

Now the father [of Schreber] was no insignificant person. . . . His activities in favour of promoting the harmonious upbringing of the young, of securing co-ordination between education in the home and in the school, of introducing physical culture and manual work with a view of raising the standards of health – all this exerted a lasting influence upon his contemporaries (p. 51).

Freud cites this information about the father to show how he was a suitable figure for 'transfiguration into a God in the affectionate memory of the son from whom he had been so early separated by death' (p. 51). (Schreber was actually nineteen years old when his father died.) It is clear from these remarks that Freud assumes that the early relationship between Schreber and his father was a loving or affectionate one; indeed, it is precisely this love that menaces the patient and brings on the psychosis. As we shall see shortly, this description of the father fits the image he presented to his family and the world, but not the way he actually treated his children.

Freud's rather naive attitude toward the father's authority represents the persistence of conventional male-centered values.

For, following his own rules for decoding the delusional beliefs, one could as easily assume that Schreber was abused and mistreated by his father, since he continually feels himself abused and mistreated by Flechsig and God. Freud's failure to interpret Schreber's beliefs in this way is similar to his shift away from the seduction-trauma theory of neurosis to the theory that inculpates the child's impulses, wishes and fantasies. In other words, both shy away from criticism of conventional authority. If we apply the *symbolic transformation* hypothesis discussed in the last chapter, we could guess that Schreber's relationship with his father – like that of Anna O., Katharina and Dora with their fathers – contained significant real traumatic experiences which are symbolically displayed in the symptoms of his adult disturbance. But this is not the course that Freud took in his analysis of Schreber; rather, he exculpates the father and places the major causal role on the son's sexual impulses, just as he did in the construction of his metapsychological explanation of the 'hysterical' women.

Freud's explanation of how Schreber's sexual impulses brought on his psychosis is a complicated one though at its center is a single cause: a disruptive, 'feminine' sexuality. In Freud's terms this is the pathological role of 'latent homosexuality' in paranoia. Two elements of Schreber's case are of central significance in this respect: the conviction that he has a role to play as a religious redeemer and the belief that he must be transformed from a man to a woman. Freud hypothesizes that the first idea is a defense against the second: that Schreber is threatened by his passive homosexual impulses (the wish to be a woman) and defends against them with grandiose fantasies. Eventually, these defensive efforts become the religious delusional system where his 'latent homosexuality' becomes a virtue, a moral necessity required to save the world. Freud's explanation runs as follows: (1) Schreber's 'homosexual libido' becomes active, manifesting itself in the dream-like thought that 'it really must be rather pleasant to be a woman succumbing to intercourse' ('Memoirs,' p. 63) – a thought that actually came to Schreber before his second breakdown. Freud can only guess why the homosexual libido appears when it does; he thinks it may be due to Schreber's wife's absence on vacation at the time (the missing heterosexual outlet) or their failure to have children, thus depriving him of a son as a male love object.   (2) The aroused homosexual feelings and fantasies are threatening and, in defending against this threat, projection and the mechanisms of paranoia are brought into play.   (3) Freud outlines this paranoid-defensive process as a series of propositions that summarize what occurs in the patient: the proposition 'I (a man) love him' (the basic homosexual wish) is contradicted by delusions of persecution – 'I do not *love* him – I *hate* him', further transformed and justified as 'I do not *love* him – I *hate* him because be persecutes me.' Thus an internal threat (homosexual libido) is transformed into an external threat (ideas of persecution). In sum: Freud posits that Schreber was sexually attracted to Flechsig, his male psychiatrist and, before him, to his father, and that he defends against these feelings by transforming the homosexual impulses into the persecution by Flechsig and God.

Schreber's father

Freud limited himself to the 'Memoirs' in his analysis of Schreber. Though he knew who the father was in a general way, he makes no use of, and presumably did not know anything about, the particulars of the father's ideas. We are now in the fortunate position of having a good deal more evidence about the father. William Niederland, an American psychoanalyst, has done extensive research on the case, interviewing relevant individuals in Europe and bringing to light the significance of the father's many books dealing with physical culture, medical treatment and childrearing. Niederland is apparently the first to draw attention to the connections between Schreber's delusional ideas and the father's prescriptions for the treatment of children. [6]

Daniel Paul Schreber's father was Daniel Gottlieb Moritz Schreber, a physician and educator of great influence in German-speaking countries in the nineteenth century. He authored numerous books concerned with physical and moral health, books that prescribed techniques for the raising of children from infancy to adulthood. The titles give the flavor: 'The Harmful Body Positions and Habits of Children, Including a Statement of Counteracting Measures'; 'The Cold Water Healing Method'; and 'The Book of Health of the Art of Living According to the Arrangement and the Rules of Human Nature'. His most popular work, 'Medical Indoor Gymnastics', went through forty editions and was translated into several languages. I will refer to the father as 'Doctor' Schreber hereafter - the son was also a doctor, of jurisprudence, but the title fits the father better. He was a physician and self-styled medical expert: a man concerned with fixing, molding, and shaping the human body, with eliminating all that he considered base, weak, and sinful.

Doctor Schreber had very definite ideas concerning the treatment of children. These are detailed in his many books and both Niederland and Schatzman assume, given the Doctor's thoroughness and other evidence, that he carefully supervised the upbringing of his own children (including Daniel Paul) according to these principles. Given this assumption, we can recreate the childhood experiences of the son from the father's writings and use this new information to illuminate the son's 'nervous illness' and the meaning of the 'Memoirs.'

Like so many other experts in the history of Western Civilization, Doctor Schreber thought his age was 'soft,' 'decadent,' and 'morally weak.' This was due to a lack of firmness and discipline in the home and school and the Doctor proposed an elaborate system of childrearing to 'battle the weakness' of his era. He was a devout Christian and all he counseled was phrased in a language of 'God' and 'love.' His proposals were always for the

child's own good and aimed at eradicating base or evil impulses
so that the child would grow in the Right, Just, and True
manner. When we view his methods today, he seems to demand
complete submission of the child to adult authority and to punish,
quite harshly, any sign of sexuality.

Two quotations from Doctor Schreber will give the flavor of
his ideas and values:

The noble seeds of human nature sprout upwards in their
purity almost on their own if the ignoble ones, the weeds,
are sought out and destroyed in time. This must be done
ruthlessly and vigorously. It is a dangerous error to believe
that flaws in a child's character will disappear by themselves.
The blunt edges may disappear but the root remains, shows
itself in poisoned impulses, and has a damaging effect on the
noble tree of life. A child's misbehavior will become in the
adult a serious fault in character and opens the way to vice
and baseness. . . . especially important and crucial for the
whole life with regard to character . . . to form a protective
wall against the unhealthy predominance of the emotional side,
against that feeble sensitiveness – the disease of our age,
which must be recognized as the usual reason for the increasing frequency of depression, mental illness, and suicide (as
quoted in Schatzman, 1973, pp. 19-20).

These quotations reveal that the 'weeds' that Doctor Schreber
is concerned to stamp out of the child have to do with feelings –
'the emotional side . . . feeble sensitiveness'; in other words,
with the maternal, female, and childlike aspects of human nature.
His methods are directed against such feelings, including
sexuality and masturbation, though like many nineteenth-century
moralists, he could not mention these by name. His disciplinary
efforts are also directed at the child's 'will.' He states, 'suppress
everything in the child, keep everything away from him that he
should not make his own, and guide him perseveringly towards
everything to which he should habituate himself' (quoted in
Schatzman, p. 20).

In the methods of child care he advocates, Doctor Schreber
exemplifies the 'new' – nineteenth-century-Christian-enlightened-
scientific spirit. The underlying values – the view of emotion,
pleasure and sexuality as threatening components of human
nature that parents need battle, and the idea that the child's
will must be combated with strong discipline – were not new,
of course. One sees these values and beliefs quite clearly in the
preceding centuries of European family life. Nor is it novel to
justify almost any mode of child treatment (or abuse) in the name
of God, Christianity, Morality, the Good, the True, and the
Beautiful. But there are several aspects of the Doctor's approach
that are new, and these are worth noting.

First, the Doctor counsels a very early attack on the child's
will: where the experts of prior centuries were content to ignore
this area until around the age of two, he argues that the battle
must be joined almost from the beginning of life and be waged on

all fronts. For example, in discussing the way to handle very
young infants, the Doctor advises:

> Our entire effect on the direction of the child's will at this
> time will consist in accustoming it to absolute obedience, which
> has been in great part prepared for already by the applica-
> tions of principles laid down previously. . . . The thought
> should never occur to the child that his will could be in control,
> rather should the habit of subordinating his will to the will of
> his parents or teachers be immutably implanted in him. . . .
> There is then joined to the feeling of law a feeling of impos-
> sibility of struggling against the law; a child's obedience, the
> basic condition for all further education, is thus solidly
> founded for the time to come (quoted in Schatzman, pp. 21-2).

Where earlier authorities were content to let a little autonomy
and will flourish – indeed, it was often stimulated by teasing and
purposeful frustrations – before battling it, Doctor Schreber
attempts to forestall its very appearance.

A second novel feature of the Doctor's approach is the use
of all sorts of mechanical devices and contraptions that are
applied to the child to mold, strengthen, and moralize his body.
The Doctor is the Thomas Edison of childcare machines. There
are belts to tie children in one position while they sleep, metal
bars to keep them sitting straight, harnesses and springs to
pull the shoulders back, and straps that bind the head and keep
it upright by pulling on the hair. The Doctor obviously did not
believe that the human body could move, sit, stand, or lie down
in the 'correct' way without mechanical assistance. We have but
to imagine ourselves as young children tied rigidly in bed or
made to sit for hours in a fixed position, to realize how painful
and oppressive these techniques were. An additional specially
harmful feature of such devices was the way in which their inter-
position between parent and child interfered with the mutual
communication of emotion. A father who twists his child's arm
is directly aware of the pain he inflicts and may be influenced
by the child's cries. If the child is strapped into a bed by a
'scientific' instrument, the parent does not so directly feel the
pain he is causing. The machine separates him from his own
potential empathy. Doctor Schreber's machines for child-shaping
are homely examples of devices we know on a much wider scale
in modern warfare – for example, the pilot who does not feel
empathy for the victims of his bombs because distance, speed,
and radar are interposed between his actions and their effects
on the victims.

A third novel feature of the Doctor's approach is the extension of discipline from behavior to the mind. The child must not
only outwardly obey and engage in the right acts, his obedience
must extend inward – he must always think the right thoughts
as well. We might say that the Doctor counsels 'thought control,'
as we have come to know it in certain modern totalitarian states.

This is a complicated issue because, in reality, mind and body
are never separated, so that the more careless brutalities of

earlier periods affected the mind of the child as well as his body. The point is that the child was not required to like it when he was whipped or abused and, further, could indulge in thoughts and fantasies or revenge or express his violence towards other children. This is certainly the picture that Hunt (1970) and others paint of seventeenth-century French life, as we saw in Chapter 2. Doctor Schreber's approach is less outwardly brutal: there is less talk of whipping and beating the child and much emphasis on 'love' and discipline in the name of God and the Natural. At the same time, what is done to the child is likely to be even more frustrating since it is imposed earlier, is mediated by mechanical devices, and extends systematically into all areas of his life. *And,* the child is made to act as if he likes what is being done to him: the Doctor counsels that children should not show 'spite' or 'bitterness' towards the adults who discipline them and must apologize and shake hands after a reprimand or punishment. Thus, the child must not only obey and submit to discipline and punishment, but must *act* as if he is not angry, and even as if he feels friendly toward his tormentor.

The Doctor's need to rationalize his own violence and the threats posed by 'softness' and disobedience is such that a system of thoroughgoing mystification is constructed. Since it is imposed on the child very early in life, when his capacity for understanding is barely formed, by a seemingly unanimous group of God-like adults, it is only natural that the child incorporate the entire system, rationalizations and all, into his own personality. Schatzman stresses this point: Doctor Schreber not only programmed his children to obey him completely, but also not to be aware of the process and its origins - to think of their obedience as their own 'free choice.' In psychoanalytic terms we see here the inculcation of a *severe unconscious superego,* the creation of an inner agency that prohibits, criticizes, and controls impulses, feelings, and fantasies, and that remains outside of awareness. This agency or part of the self is modeled on the parent-child interaction; one comes to treat aspects of oneself as these aspects were treated by the authorities of one's childhood.

Doctor Schreber's methods defined the childhood matrix in which Daniel Paul Schreber's personality was formed - including *his* severe unconscious superego and other anlage of his delusional system. Let us look in a bit more detail at the father's methods. The father counseled that love and softness not be encouraged, that the infant be rewarded when he was calm, not crying, not demanding or being willful. We do not really know what went on in the son's earliest years - general practice at the time would suggest that nurses had the day-to-day care of the infant, under the supervision of the mother and, of course the ubiquitous Doctor. Niederland (1963) quotes from a letter written by Schreber's sister that the mother worked closely with the Doctor in everything. In any case, it seems likely from the Doctor's writings that all areas of the child's life came under scrutiny and attempted control. If an infant cries for what the Doctor deems 'no reason,' it is seen as self-will which must be met with 'moderate, intermittent, bodily admonishments consistently repeated.' Here are some additional examples of the recommended methods.

Eating is subjected to strict regulation from the earliest months. Far from eating when they are hungry, infants are fed according to a schedule set by adults. They must learn great self-control with regard to food - adults eat in their presence but they are not to be given the smallest morsel, even if they cry or beg. From the age of six months, warm baths should be discontinued in favor of cold baths, along with 'cold rubbings of the body' which have a 'toughening-up' effect. Their rooms were not to be heated lest the children become soft. Along with these stringent regulations of food and body temperature were the use of the many straps, braces, harnesses, and other apparatuses for controlling the body and its movements already described. One has but to imagine himself as a young child subjected to these modes of control to see how almost all areas of potential pleasure and comfort - eating, moving, playing, even sleeping - were made painful and difficult.

The Doctor was an absolute fanatic regarding posture. He had a passionate belief in balancing all actions of the body, a sort of right-left fetish. The child was to perform all actions and movements equally with the right and left hand, arm, foot, or leg. This was related to the emphasis on straight posture and all was rationalized in the name of health and medicine. A single example:

> One must see to it that children always sit straight and even-sided on both buttocks at once . . . leaning neither to the right nor left side. . . . As soon as they start to lean back . . . or bend their backs, the time has come to exchange at least for a few minutes the seated position for the absolutely still, supine one. . . . If this is not done . . . the back bones will be deformed. . . . *Half resting in lying or wallowing positions* should not be allowed: If children are awake they should be alert and hold themselves in straight, active positions and be busy; in general each thing that could lead towards laziness and softness (for example the sofa in the children's room) should be kept away from their circle of activity (Schatzman, p. 44).

This concern with management of the child's body was, no doubt, extended to those other areas that the Doctor could not directly mention by name - sex, masturbation, urination, and defecation, with their various pleasurable, soft, dirty, sensuous, and degenerate connotations. (The Doctor, and his son, like most nineteenth-century authorities, referred to emissions of semen as 'pollutions.') And in these areas too, we can be sure that control and strict discipline was justified in the name of medical necessity, health, and the child's own well-being.

As the children became older, the Doctor recommended the use of a 'punishment board.' All transgressions of the many family rules and regulations were to be written down on a board in the child's room so that he would be constantly reminded of his sins. The entire family would then gather before the board, once a week, for a meting out of praise and admonitions by the father.[7]

The father's methods and the son's psychosis
We come now to the specific parallels and connections between these methods – which we can assume were applied to Schreber by his father – and his adult psychotic experiences, and specifically the belief system outlined in the 'Memoirs.' As an overall statement the effects of the Doctor's methods on his son may be understood in two stages, corresponding to the 'pre-psychotic' and 'psychotic' stages in Schreber's life.

First and foremost, the Doctor's methods worked: his son's will was outwardly crushed – 'soul murder' is his phrase in the 'Memoirs' – and he became an extremely obedient, scrupulous, hard-working, self-denying individual. Studies of the effects of terror, for example in police states and concentration camps and especially examples where these methods are applied early in life, demonstrate the pervasive and long-lasting effects of such traumas. Persons subjected to terror remain terrified, usually for life; they go to great lengths to avoid repetition of the tortures they have experienced. Such experiences also leave a legacy of depression and self-destructive tendencies. Concentration camp survivors speak of the wish to kill themselves to avoid reexperiencing the horrors that continue to haunt them years after they have left the camp. Severe depression was a prominent feature of Schreber's two breakdowns, as were numerous attempts to kill himself. His older brother, who was raised by the same methods, suffered from depression and committed suicide by shooting himself at the age of thirty-eight. Thus, the first effect of the father's child-rearing regime was to create a son who internalized the values embodied in the father's methods. He became a 'good,' frightened boy and, as an adult, was extremely eager to please and comply with authority, as attested by his rapid success as a judge in the authoritarian German legal system. As far as we can tell, the mystifications and rationalizations of the father's methods were effective: during this first or prepsychotic stage, Schreber revered his father and other male authorities – including God. Bad feelings, depression, bodily aches and pains, and suicidal acts were experienced as ego-alien; they were attributed to 'fatigue' or some other cause external to the self.

The second stage, Schreber's psychosis proper, may be understood as the breakup of the personality compliant with the internalized rules of his father. It was a revolt against the tyranny experienced as a child – a tyranny that had continued within the adult personality. In other words, the seemingly bizarre aspects of the delusional system described in the 'Memoirs' become understandable when we view them as a symbolic re-experiencing of the traumas of childhood. Schreber must regress to his painful childhood in order to free himself from the long-lasting effects of his·traumatic upbringing, effects enshrined in his harsh, unconscious superego – the sadistic father within his adult self.

The major key to the translation of the 'Memoirs' is the sub-stitution of 'father' for 'God' and 'childrearing method' for 'miracle.' The overall scheme of the 'psychotic' belief system – that God's rays are drawn to his body and keep interfering with its functions in a loving-punishing way – is then seen as a symbolic description of what he experienced as a child under the Doctor's sadistic-intrusive care. Drawing on Niederland and Schatzman, we may examine some specific examples.

Schreber writes, '*Miracles of heat and cold* were and still are daily enacted against me . . . always with the purpose of prevent-ing the natural feelings of bodily well-being.' This represents the father's 'Cold-Water Healing Method,' the use of cold baths and cold rubbings from infancy onward, and no heat in the child's bedroom.

The son describes 'the so-called coccyx miracle . . . an extremely painful, caries-like state of the lowest vertebrae. Its purpose was *to make sitting and even lying down impossible*.' He goes on to describe how he 'was not allowed to remain for long in one and the same position . . . when I was walking one attempted to force me to lie down, and when I was lying down one wanted to chase me off my bed.' The 'ones' that do this to the adult Schreber are God's 'rays,' which are inside his body, that is, his superego or internalized version of the father's treatment. This experience matches the father's rules and pro-cedures for enforcing 'correct' posture and preventing 'laziness' and 'wallowing' positions. The plaintive voice of the harassed little boy is heard in Schreber's statement, 'Rays [of God] did not seem to appreciate at all that a human being who actually exists must be somewhere.' (All quotations to follow are from Chapter 4 of Schatzman.)

The effects of the father's mechanical devices are experienced by the adult Schreber as the various painful bodily states caused by God's miraculous rays. There are '*tearing and pulling pains*' in his head, representations of the sensations caused by the father's straps which pulled on the hair to keep the head erect. He describes the 'compression-of-the-chest miracle' that matches the feelings of the metal bar used to keep children sitting straight at tables and desks.

A number of other aspects of Schreber's experiences may be translated as versions of the traumas of his childhood. He speaks of 'God's writing down method' which matches his father's 'punishment board.' The various disturbances in digestion and evacuation – the 'miracles' performed on his stomach and other organs – are tied to the father's rules and control over eating, urination and defecation.

The father's overall intrusive control of his son's body and its function is nicely captured in this statement from the 'Memoirs':

God is inseparably tied to my person through my nerves' power of attraction which for some time past has been inescapable; there is no possibility of God freeing Himself from my nerves for the rest of my life ('Memoirs,' p. 209).

As this passage indicates, Schreber senses that his father was drawn to interfere with his body by some powerful need of his own. In the early stages of his breakdown he speaks of God's 'play with human beings,' of God's intent to 'use him' like a 'strumpet' or 'whore,' of voices that call him 'Miss Schreber' in a sexually derogatory way. He keeps trying to understand why these painful things happened to him, why was God – his God-like father – of all Beings so involved in a sadistic manner with the body of one insignificant creature? The 'Memoirs' is a search for an explanation and an attempt to find a justification for the pain he suffered.

These examples are informative on several counts. First, they show that the father's methods were indeed a painful torture for the child who was still suffering the effects fifty years later. Second, they show the lasting mystification. The effects are mediated by an internal agency – 'God the father' is inside the son's mind and body – but Schreber does not know or under-stand what is happening to him. His breakdown, the psychosis, and the eventual writing of the 'Memoirs,' are his attempt to understand and find some meaning in all these puzzling experi-ences.

When he first breaks down, he and his doctor think he is ill ('hypochondriac'). Then all becomes confusion and chaos as he sinks into a wild and withdrawn psychotic state. Then it is Flechsig persecuting him and, finally, he discovers it was God: 'It occurred to me only much later, in fact only while writing this essay did it become quite clear to me that God Himself must have known of the plan, if indeed he was not the instigator, to commit soul murder on me' ('Memoirs,' p. 38). The chapter of the 'Memoirs' dealing with the Schreber family was censored by the court and denied publication. Because of this we will never know what Schreber said about his father there. In published portions he at times seems to implicate his father. For example, in speaking of Flechsig, he says, 'You, like so many doctors, could not completely resist the temptation of using a patient . . . as an object for . . . experiments' (p. 34).

The symbolism of so much of the 'Memoirs' comes very close to identifying the real Doctor behind God's rays, but Schreber does not take this final step, attesting to the last power of the rationalizations and mystifications that were part of the treat-ment he received as a child. I think Schreber also avoids some additional pain by not directly recognizing that his own father did these horrible things to him; he hopes and longs for love, and its lack is an excruciating part of his suffering. Thus, the

ambivalence toward God, the symbolic father, that runs throughout the 'Memoirs' (the sarcasm of 'miracles,' God's stupidity and
inability to understand living persons, being a 'whore' to God,
and the eventual transformation into a woman) is truly a state
of opposed feelings. The indirect hostility is there and so is the
intense longing for love from the father figure. It was Freud who
first noted this ambivalence, and this brings us back to a consideration of his ideas regarding Schreber's paranoia.

Freud's analysis in the light of new evidence
Freud reasoned that Schreber's feelings of persecution by God
arose from his passive-feminine impulses, his wish to assume a
female position vis-à-vis his father. There is a certain truth to
this, as the foregoing discussion should have shown. Schreber
did wish - indeed desperately longed for - the love of his father.
And this longing was unacceptable to him. Until the time of his
breakdown at age fifty-one, he was committed to the standards
of his upbringing which viewed such feelings as soft, degenerate,
and unmanly. But the evidence just reviewed casts a different
light on this conflict than that shed by Freud's interpretation.
Freud believed that such impulses were *intrinsically threatening*:
in this respect he shared the viewpoint of the Doctor and Schreber's
own prepsychotic superego. I don't mean to imply that Freud was
a Gestapo-parent like Doctor Schreber, nor that he would have
approved of the latter's methods, but simply that he shared the
general view of instinct, sexuality, and autonomous strivings.
All were seen as potential threats to the organism, in need of
control. The evidence we have just examined, on the other hand,
suggests an *iatrogenic* explanation for Schreber's insanity.
    What was threatening to Schreber was not his 'latent homo-
sexuality,' but the realization - in body and mind - that his soul
had been murdered, that his will and spirit had been broken and
torture inflicted on his body. He comes to the realization - in a
symbolic way to be sure - that his father, believing in the evil
nature of softness, comfort, pleasure, maternal love, and
individual autonomy had systematically attempted to destroy
these aspects of his soul. By 'iatrogenic' I mean that the 'disease' -
Schreber's psychosis - is not caused by his impulses (latent
homosexuality, passive-feminine wishes), but by the childrearing
methods based on the belief that such impulses were dangerous.
In a sense, he suffers from his culture's distorted view of
femininity and autonomy as this view was transmitted to him
through his father's beliefs and methods. What breaks through
when Schreber becomes psychotic is, thus, the denied and
repressed side of his humanity: femininity, softness, the desire
to feel some comfort and pleasure in his body, and his long-
repressed willfulness or autonomy.
    Freud goes astray in his explanation of the cause of Schreber's
psychosis - attributing it to the threatening quality of love
(homosexual libido) - because of the persistence of conventional
values in his theories. In addition he seems too ready to see the

father as loving, and to attribute conflict in the father-son
relationship to the son's impulses, rather than the father's
actions. This brings us to a critical point regarding Freud's
analysis. In the throes of his psychotic breakdown, and in the
complications of the system he develops in the 'Memoirs,' Schreber
is struggling to understand and tell the world something of great
importance about fathers and children; about love, masculinity,
and femininity; about discipline and child abuse. He is struggling
to express these ideas in a society dominated by men, by fathers,
and by a male God. While Freud's analysis illuminates a great
deal about Schreber, it misses these essential issues.

Let me conclude with an integrated summary of the Schreber
case, a summary that will, I hope, complete the transition from
conventional values to the new psychoanalytic world view.

Schreber's transformation: a synthesis
We must begin our attempt to understand Schreber, not with his
psychosis, but with a critical examination of his 'normality.' With
a few exceptions, those who have written on the case, including
Freud, accept this normality at face value. Yet what does it
mean to call a life like this normal? What was Schreber like during
the forty-two years before his first acknowledged breakdown?
His wide knowledge and achievements as a lawyer and judge
indicate that he was an excellent student, a willing pupil who
absorbed much during his school years. Dedicated to hard work
and extremely self-denying, Schreber did not marry until the
age of thirty-six. His wife was a sickly woman (diabetic according
to Kitay, 1963) who was fifteen years younger than he. They had
a very close relationship and Schreber always spoke of her in
loving and respectful terms. Indeed, he first undertook the
writing of the 'Memoirs' to acquaint her with the oddities of his
behavior prior to his return from the hospital. They were persistently disappointed in their attempts to have children; his
wife underwent six, full-term stillbirths. There is much symbolic
material in the 'Memoirs' dealing with the illustrious Schreber
family line that no doubt relates to this. The failure to have
children was, by Schreber's own account, a sharp disappointment.

He was quite successful in his profession; he rose to a high
judicial position - more or less equivalent to chief justice in a
court of appeal in our system - at what was apparently a young
age. From this, we can assume he made a favorable impression
on the officials and other judges with whom he worked. His
professional accomplishments, and the feeling one gets from the
'Memoirs,' suggest a man who outwardly manifested the virtues
of his society: a tremendous capacity for hard work, rectitude,
and compliance with the rules and laws of the system. He was,
after all, *a judge*: an official embodiment of social conscience or
superego, an interpreter and enforcer of standards and laws.

In sum, the 'normal' Schreber was a shining example of his
father's principles in action. He was self-denying, 'moral' to a
fault, an extremely hard worker (none of that 'laziness' or

'wallowing' on sofas), obedient to authority, and possessed of tremendous sexual inhibitions. 'Few people have been brought up according to such strict moral principles as I, and have throughout life practiced such moderation especially in matters of sex, as I venture to claim for myself' ('Memoirs,' p. 208) he states, and I think we can believe him. Not only did his personal life and habits show the harsh superego in action, but in his career he was, like his suicidal brother before him, a judge: a representative of social or national superego. Schreber, along with his countrymen who revered the father and bought so many editions of his books, considered this a virtuous, manly, and admirable way to live.

What is wrong with this view of the normal life? The Doctor's own approach, because it is so exaggerated, highlights the bizarre ideas associated with this sort of normality. For is it not a bit crazy to equate morality and virtue with extreme sexual self-denial? What can it mean to think of semen, the human seed necessary to propagate life, as a pollution, as some kind of garbage? What is 'moral' about the interference with so many species-wide processes – body movement, eating, defecating, sexual pleasure, sleeping, and posture? Obviously, the values and practices that we see in the Doctor's approach are a caricature of the patriarchal state, with its attack on all that seems feminine, maternal, 'soft' and autonomous. And it is the rigid and unbalanced nature of this attack that makes this sort of normality so abnormal, so out of phase with human nature, or, as Schreber himself puts it in the 'Memoirs,' how God's actions are not in keeping with 'the Order of the World,' or 'the Order of Things.'

In Schreber's personal version of this abnormal-normality, life must have been a constant struggle to maintain a rigid control. He would be forced to repress and in other ways keep from consciousness all those feelings, urges, and memories that conflicted with his internalized version of the moral, normal life. Sexual impulses of all sorts, including the most rudimentary longings for love, pleasure, and body comfort – could he lie down? dare he relax his posture? touch his wife's body – must be squelched. Then there would be the immense store of frustration and rage aroused by the sadistic father and potentially active in relation to later 'fathers' – judges, officials, doctors, God – as well as in relation to the 'father' within himself. Mingled with these would be willfulness and urges toward autonomy, the revolutionary spirit and wish to break free from repressive authority – both external and internal. And, finally, would be the repressed memories of all the pain he suffered as a child, all the perplexing, 'loving' punishments, the sadistic intrusions and violent manipulations of his body. To function in an acceptable way, Schreber would have been forced to dissociate all these feelings, wishes, and memories from the conscious version of his 'normal' self. They made up the content of his unconscious, the dissociated or repressed side of his personality.

We come, now, to the details of Schreber's psychosis. Why, having functioned successfully for a number of years, does he finally make such a sharp break with reality and plunge into the painful world of madness? Freud suggests that it is due to the breakthrough of homosexual libido. Schreber himself attributes it – initially – to the overwork occasioned by his new job. Of course, in his later versions, he sees it as due to his persecution by Flechsig, by God, and all the other miraculous circumstances outlined in the 'Memoirs.' A number of later psychoanalytic writers have pointed to possible precipitating factors including: his loss of the election for the Reichstag, his reaching the same age – fifty-one – at which his father suffered a head injury that led to his deterioration and subsequent death (an 'anniversary reaction'), and the failure to have children. This last must have been specially painful, since his wife repeatedly went through a full pregnancy only to deliver a dead baby. For one predisposed to believe that his semen was a pollution, this must have seemed a striking confirmation of guilt and inner evil.

All of these factors no doubt added to the stress that led to Schreber's breakdown, though it is not really possible to know how important each one actually was. There is a danger, however, that speculations about such precipitating factors will obscure the main issue. Like the question of Schreber's 'normality,' the question of what precipitated the psychosis should be turned around. In the light of what we now know about his life, the question to ask is, 'How did he function for so many years without breaking down earlier?' In other words, the mystery is not why be became insane but how he remained 'normal' given his earlier experiences. Part of the answer to this question is again to be found in his society's view of normality. From the bits of evidence available, it seems likely that Schreber's unconscious conflicts appeared as depression and 'sickness' at various earlier points in his life. The first breakdown, and the beginning phase of the second, were both labeled hypochondria – there was sleep disturbance and various bodily complaints. Everyone was only too ready to see these symptoms as due to some unspecified physical illness, to be treated by medicine. (At the time of the second breakdown, Flechsig promised Schreber a cure with a new sleeping medication, much as psychosis is treated in the mental hospitals of today; times change and they stay the same!) As long as Schreber remained compliant with the values of his society – as long as he was the respectable, hard-working, and obedient lawyer and judge – the signs of his internal distress were attributed to factors apart from his personality and way of life. In this way, both he and his doctors avoided the threat aroused by relating 'symptoms' to the person and his mode of living.

To restate this point in a different form: the explanation one formulates to explain Schreber's psychosis – whether precipitating factors or its overall meaning – stems from a paradigm, theory, or world view. One explanation will be given if the world view is

that shared by Schreber's fellow citizens, by his father, by
Flechsig, and even, in certain ways, by Freud. Within this
view, Schreber's 'normality' is not questioned and the cause
of the psychosis is sought in various external agents: his bad
sexual habits, his homosexual libido, overwork and sleep loss,
or even such apparently psychoanalytic factors as an 'anniversary reaction.' A very different explanation will be given from
a point of view that takes a critical stance relative to the values
of this society. Within this framework, the psychosis is seen as
a personal-moral crisis, an overthrow of the internal values of
'normal' society. From this perspective, Schreber's own rather
simple-appearing explanation for the onset of his second breakdown – that it was brought on by too much hard work on his
new job in a strange city where he and his wife had few friends
and little social life – gets closer to the truth, especially as one
considers the deeper meaning of work and pleasure in the family-
social context of Schreber's life. Let us here follow the course of
the second breakdown from this critical perspective.

Schreber and his wife move to a new city, Dresden, so that he
can assume his post as chief judge. He finds a 'heavy burden of
work' and, with his characteristic fairness, wonders whether it
was 'personal ambition' that drove him to work so hard. This may
have been a part of it, but he is more certain that he was
anxious to earn 'respect among my colleagues and others concerned
with the Court . . . by unquestionable efficiency.' The other
judges were all older than he, which made him, by his own account,
even more anxious to do a good job, to impress them with his
'efficiency.' In addition to all this work, there was no fun, no
play.

> There was almost no opportunity for social distraction which
> would certainly have been much better for me – this became
> evident to me when I slept considerably better after the only
> occasion on which we had been asked to a dinner party – but
> we hardly knew anybody in Dreden ('Memoirs,' p. 64).

So there were no more dinner parties, no social distractions, and
the first symptoms of disturbance – inability to sleep and 'crackling noises' in the walls which kept waking him up (in retrospect
he sees these as divine messages) – appear. I think his state at
this time can be described as follows: the normal Schreber,
operating according to the deeply-ingrained superego, works
hard, is fearful of displeasing the authorities, strives to earn
their respect, and so on and on in a never-ending fashion. The
rewards for such obedient performance were never much in the
way of direct pleasure or fun. There were the rewards of higher
positions, but these, while gratifying, also meant a further
burden of work. Given what we know of his upbringing, it is
reasonable to assume that a superego such as his would never be
satisfied: there would always be more demands and ever more
impulses to fight back. This burden of work and conscience might
have been balanced by the pleasures of children or friends –
relationships that gave expression to his need for love and to the

maternal side of his nature but, as we know, these were notably absent. The sixth miscarriage and his advancing age made it clear that there would be no children to love and be loved by; no friends in the new city, and not even any dinner parties! In other words, his outward circumstances portrayed, in exaggerated form, the substance of his entire life: obedience, efficiency, hard work, renunciation – all the masculine virtues – and little care, tenderness or love. The never-ending internal demands and constrictions, together with the further lack of love and pleasure, combined to create a crisis, as they had on several earlier occasions. His laboriously maintained outward personality begins to crack apart (is that the shell of his obedient self that he projects into the crackling walls?). Symptoms – at first sleeplessness – overtake him and force him to leave his new post in Dresden and to return to Flechsig for treatment (by way of his mother's house, interestingly enough).

The treatment, largely drugs and other attempts to help him sleep, proves ineffective. He grows increasingly suspicious of Flechsig, another 'doctor' who tells 'white lies' and experiments on his body, as he notes in the 'Memoirs.' The crisis deepens and he sinks into the madness that is to consume him over the next years, a madness that he experiences as 'the end of the world' – the end of his normal self – and from which he eventually extricates himself by creating a new world – a new self – expressed in the revelations of the 'Memoirs.' Most striking, of course, is the central necessity that this new self be in part feminine, with an acceptance, indeed a welcoming, of the feelings of pleasure that Schreber associates with that state.

What I am suggesting is essentially this: Schreber's self – including his body with all its built-in postural rules, strictures condemning all sensual pleasure, in short, the self with its punitive, unconscious father within – becomes an intolerably painful burden. This self must be destroyed, at first by becoming sick, and then totally incapacitated and insane. Once destroyed, there is the possibility of reconstruction, and this begins as Schreber engages in a war with God and His absurd rules. The chaotic insanity becomes focused around the struggle to get God out of his body, to overthrow His (God-father-superego) tyranny, and to create a new set of rules – a new religion or moral code. This new code allows, even demands, that there be a place for his feminine-maternal and autonomous qualities.

How does this interpretation of Schreber's psychosis differ from others that have been offered? Many who have written about the case are, like Freud, still trapped within the conventional world view. Within that view the psychosis, the breakdown, the loss of ability to function in the old or normal way are seen as signs of sickness: badness or evil if one is religiously inclined, psychosis or schizophrenia to the medically or scientifically trained. I am suggesting an alternative view: that the initial breakdown occurs because of the confluence of factors that make

Schreber's normal life intolerable. Next comes a chaotic, dis-
organized, frightening, painful and confusing state in which he
passively suffers the effects of his conflicts. Gradually, this
suffering takes an active form as he identifies what is wrong: it
is Flechsig and then God, and all the one-sided values that God
espouses. Once the problem is given this definition, Schreber
can fight against it, reconstruct his personality and attempt to
communicate, through his book, the wider meaning of his
experience.

When we consider Schreber's breakdown and transformation in
this way, as a creative struggle for freedom, it can be termed a
form of self-therapy. [8] But how is therapy carried on without a
therapist? Since there is no analyst to serve as a transference
figure, Schreber uses first Flechsig and then the God of his
delusional world. In order to free himself from his internal
tyrant he must have some way of 'seeing it' apart from himself.
He struggles to separate himself from his internal father by
projecting it into the outside world: it is not he persecuting
himself, but Flechsig and then God. The projection is a necessary -
though terrifying - part of the process by which his old personality is destroyed, making way for a new self. When viewed
in this way, the constant threats to 'unman' him, reported in
the 'Memoirs', do not refer to homosexual impulses; they are,
rather, part of the struggle with the rigid patriarchal superego,
a struggle to define his feminine qualities as desirable rather
than repugnant. By projecting the various aspects of his superego outside himself, Schreber is able to engage in a form of
combat and, eventually, to expose the absurdity of its rules.

But to do so he must regress, he must recapture the state of
potential autonomy he had as a boy. *In order to break free from
his extremely punitive superego, he must lift the repression
surrounding its origin and reexperience the tortures and pain of
his childhood.* This is precisely what happens during the florid
phase of his psychosis; he goes to war with God and struggles
against Him and all His tortures and absurd rules. This struggle
contains the various ambivalent feelings toward the father and
the self. Part of him attempts to comply and be loved, while
another part rebels. Here is a single example illustrating the
struggle over posture and body position, together with a
characteristic comment on God:

I mainly sat *motionless* the whole day on a chair at my table . . .
even in the garden I preferred to remain seated in the same
spot. . . . I considered absolute passivity almost a religious
duty. . . . Although this idea did not originate spontaneously
in me but was induced by the voices that talked to me. I kept
it up myself for a time until I realized it was purposeless. That
rays could ever expect me to remain totally immobile . . .
['not the slightest movement' was an oft-repeated slogan] must
be connected, I am convinced, with God not knowing how to
treat a living human being, as He was accustomed to dealing
only with corpses ('Memoirs,' p. 127).

We see, in this example, Schreber carrying the father's postural restrictions to an extreme which reveals their absurdity. Those who saw Schreber during his later, posthospitalization phase, reported that he often held his head at a somewhat odd angle, expressing, I would think, his refusal to comply with father-God's postural rule. Once the rules are exposed in this way, he can criticize them (rays, God) and move toward a new and different way of life. But the danger – the terror – is that he does this from the standpoint of a little child, dependent on parental love and frightened of punishment. This is, of course, symbolized in the image of one puny man in combat with God. On a larger scale, this is what he did through the years of his psychotic struggles. He shows, through his personal experience, how God's way of treating people is painful and nonsensical. God is out of phase with 'the Order of the World,' an oft-repeated message in the 'Memoirs.' This is, in my view, the redeeming message that Schreber is trying to communicate to his fellow citizens. His father's and his society's sadistic treatment of children, and their rigid and repressive standards of adult conduct, are contrary to human nature, to 'the Order of Things.' They are fine for corpses or machines, but harmful to living beings.

This redeeming message is then given the most concrete personal expression in the idea that he, Schreber, must be transformed into a woman. This transformation, which he believes is necessary for both his personal salvation and the salvation of the world, is a powerful symbolic statement of the need to reassert the value of the female-maternal side of life – of tenderness, care, and love – in the face of the masculine-Prussian standards represented by his father's beliefs and methods.

In sum, Schreber's struggle is a moral one, in the traditional meaning of that term; it is his attempt to shape a new code of life, a new superego, that will give a more adequate expression to all sides of human nature. The fact that he had to descend to the depths of insanity in order to destroy the old order attests to the degree of its one-sidedness and rigidity. A concluding quotation from the 'Memoirs' illustrates, in quite a poignant way, much that I have been trying to say. Schreber is describing how things will be in his transformed state. When this state is reached, God will have reversed the nature of his demands:

> God demands a *constant state of enjoyment*, such as would be in keeping with the conditions of existence imposed upon souls by the Order of Things; and it is my duty to provide Him with this . . . in the shape of the greatest possible generation of spiritual voluptuousness. And if, in this process, a little sensual pleasure falls to my share, I feel justified in accepting it as some slight compensation for the inordinate measure of suffering and privation that has been mine for so many past years (As quoted in Freud, 1911, p. 34).

The interesting fact is that once he had symbolically transformed himself into a female being, Schreber showed the qualities of a loving mother and not a male homosexual.[9] Niederland has interviewed some of those who knew Schreber during the period after his release from confinement, including an orphaned young girl that the Schrebers adopted in 1903. It was Schreber's idea to adopt her and he was 'more of a mother to me than my mother.' Niederland continues:

> She [the adopted daughter] also gave me letters and poems written by Schreber, details on his personal warmth and kindness, told me how he helped her with her school work, took her on hikes through the forests and mountains surrounding Dresden, and so on. These additional data coincide with information from other sources. Schreber's letters and poetry disclose his personal sensitivity and a quality of genuine tenderness, over and above that creative ability which found expression in the writing of the 'Memoirs' (1974, pp. 31-2).

This detailed analysis of Schreber has shown, I hope, how the belief system of the 'Memoirs' is, in its idiosyncratic way, aligned with the new world view of psychoanalysis. While Freud's analysis of Schreber only partly captured that aspect of the case, due to his lingering commitment to conventional values, his own views continued their progressive journey. In his later works – most clearly in 'Civilization and its Discontents' – he arrives at a position quite close to that which I have outlined in the foregoing synthesis of the Schreber case. It is to this essay that we may now turn.

6 AGGRESSION, DEATH AND THE DISCONTENTS OF CIVILIZATION

As Freud moved into the final decade of his life, he increasingly turned his attention to the broad question of the source of neurotic suffering. Why was there such a great deal of anxiety, guilt, depression, personal pain and unhappiness in a world of astonishing material progress? Why were the most civilized of persons, the successful members of the most advanced societies, so often discontented with their lives? The state of psychoanalytic theory, as Freud took up these large questions, can be described as follows: the case studies and clinical papers traced the source of neurosis to several kinds of instinct - sex, aggression, self-preservation, and to various traumas involving sexual stimulation, seductions, loss of love and of love objects, death, and the consequences of aggressive or brutal treatment. The general theory or metapsychology gave primary emphasis to sexual energy as motive and, hence, to unconscious conflicts between impulses toward sexual gratification and the forces opposing it: reality and its internalized representatives. Several attempts had been made to broaden the general theory by adding to the list of instincts and causative traumas, most notably in 'Beyond the Pleasure Principle' of 1920. A new theory of anxiety and its role in neurosis had been presented in the 1926 'Inhibitions, Symptoms and Anxiety.' Yet, in both the clinical and theoretical spheres, one still found the mixture of conventional and critical, of male-centered and bisexual, of scientistic and psychoanalytic, so characteristic of the unfinished journey.

In the essays written near the end of his long and productive career Freud was moving toward an explanation of neurotic suffering that would be largely free of the inconsistencies of the earlier works. This explanation, stated most forcefully in 'Civilization and its Discontents' (1930), derives from what I have been attempting to describe as the new psychoanalytic perspective or world view.

The major task of this chapter will be to critically discuss the explanation of modern man's unhappiness as Freud presents it in 'Civilization and its Discontents.' This can best be done by first examining the reformulation of theory in two key areas: aggression and death. We will see how the theoretical treatment of these areas - like that of sexuality and masculinity-femininity - is caught between old and new perspectives. Clarification in these two areas will make possible an understanding of the crucial roles played by aggression and death in the discontents of civilized man.

AGGRESSION

Descriptions of anger, competitiveness, envy, hatred, sadism
and masochism abound in psychoanalytic observations. It is
clear that these emotional states are connected to anxiety, guilt,
attacks on the self, symptoms and neuroses of all sorts. Such
factors are present in 'The Studies on Hysteria' and, to one
degree or another, in all the cases thereafter. Yet, from the
beginning, when the general theory is developed, anger and
aggression are left aside and sexuality becomes the central
motivational force. For more than twenty years aggression is
either left out of theory – though it remains in the clinical
accounts – or, when present, is derived from libido with the
terminology of sadism and masochism. That is, aggression is
seen as secondary to the discharge and blocked discharge of
sexual energy.

The major change in this single instinct theory is made in
'Beyond the Pleasure Principle' which, as its title suggests,
considers sources of motivation other than libidinal discharge
or pleasure seeking. 'Beyond the Pleasure Principle' is a complicated work, a mixture of brilliant insights and, in my view,
some of Freud's most flawed speculations. On the positive side,
it is a step beyond libido theory: the destructive or aggressive
instinct emerges as a force coequal with sexuality, as does the
idea of conflict between eros and destruction. Yet, even as Freud
proposes aggression as an independent instinct – a move that will
take him, in later works, toward important social criticism – he
becomes most scientistic and reductionistic, attempting to derive
aggression from what he terms the basic tendency of all living
things to return to an earlier, nonliving state. This is the
'death instinct,' a confused concept which must be examined in
a bit more detail.

Freud's reasoning behind the death instinct runs as follows:
all living things eventually die; all that is organic returns to an
inorganic state. There is, thus, a 'tendency' to repeat and a
sense in which the 'goal' of life is death. Freud points, as
example, to experiments with single-celled organisms or 'protista.'
While it is true that all living things die, this biological fact
cannot be directly translated into a motive to explain the complex
actions of human beings. This is the sort of crude reductionism
that mars Freud's thought from time to time. He uses the two
terms 'repetition' and 'death' in broad ways to form a bridge
from the biological cycle of organic to inorganic to human activities on quite a different level of analysis.

Repetition is employed in a loose and shifting manner to desig-
nate three related, but quite different, phenomena: (1) the
repetitive cycle of life to death; (2) the repetitive quality of
neurotic symptoms and patterns (the 'repetition compulsion');
and (3) mastery in which passively experienced traumas are
actively repeated. The repetition of mastery can be linked to
neurotic repetition in so far as both are attempts to adapt to

stressful or traumatic life events, though they are, of course, very different sorts of adaptation. And, it is difficult to see how mastery relates at all to return to an inorganic state. There are connections between neurotic repetition and death, and it is these that have probably given the death instinct theory its appeal. That is to say, many aspects of neurosis can be linked to death: anger and attacks on the self, as seen in masochism, depression and related states; inability to live fully or to enjoy life-related activities: especially sexuality; identifications with lost or dead persons; and, finally, suicide. In addition to these death-related aspects of neurosis, Freud's pessimistic view that certain persons seemed strongly committed to their neurotic modes of life, that they would not give them up to his psychoanalytic efforts, no matter how much pain and unhappiness they seemed to suffer, led him to speak of neurotic repetition as driven by a force so elemental that it must be something like a death instinct. Such a usage is only metaphorical, of course, and, what is more, it really explains nothing about the neurotic phenomena in question. All of the masochistic and death-related aspects of neurosis can be explained more appropriately with other psycho-analytic concepts – the powerfully motivating effects of anxiety, the complexities of identifications arising out of early, ambivalent relationships, anger and aggression – which are not the same as death – played out on an internal stage, and much more. This is not the place to describe these complex processes, Freud's own cases provide sufficient examples, as our earlier discussion has shown, and he himself never resorts to the death instinct when explaining an actual case. In sum: the equation of neurotic repetition with the return to death is a suggestive and provoca-tive metaphor but a poor explanation.

The concept of 'death' is also used in a loose and shifting manner. Thus, it refers to the fact that living things die, but this fact is then inflated to the status of a human motive, as in the 'goal of all life is death.' The idea of 'death wishes' is then used to refer to a broad range of aggressive and death-related fantasies. Somewhere in this process death and aggression become equated, and Freud then speaks of 'destruction' and a 'destructive instinct' as if aggression, death-wishes, death and the death instinct are all aspects of a single instinctual process. Like the mixed use of repetition, the equation of aggression and death, while evocative as an image, is weak as an explanation. How is this so?

Human aggression is ubiquitous, fighting sometimes becomes murderous and angry fantasies often involve the death of one's enemies. But all this does not mean that aggression and death can be equated, as the death instinct theory suggests. For, while aggression may lead to death, especially in the postindustrial age when man enacts his angry fantasies with modern weapons, it need not always do so, nor is it the case that the death of the victim is always part of aggressive motivation. Ethologists who study the fighting behavior of many animal species, including all

the primates most closely related to man, find strongly motivated
aggressive systems whose aim is to attack, hurt, frighten and
drive away other species members. But these aggressive systems
frequently include 'turn-off' actions, as in submissive gestures,
which stop such fighting short of serious injury and killing.
While the human capacity to use tools often causes our fighting
patterns to run out of control, there is no reason to believe that
our *aggressive motivation* is any different than a chimpanzee's:
we are often frustrated, angered and impelled to attack and hurt
and we sometimes kill – but this provides no basis for a biological
equivalence of aggression with death of the sort Freud proposes.

   The instinctual basis of human aggression is, itself, a very
controversial topic. But whatever position one holds with regard
to it, it is still clear that aggression and death cannot be equated:
there is a great deal of anger and fighting that is not connected
to killing and death and there is much killing and death – as in
modern warfare – seemingly unconnected to anger and aggressive
motivation. [1] It seems that whenever Freud first takes up a controversial topic such as the instinctual basis of aggression, he
turns to the kind of biologizing represented by the death instinct.
Perhaps he needed the protection afforded by the connection with
science, for we saw the same thing in his treatment of bisexuality.
Yet he is also capable of moving beyond these reductionist
versions, as he partly did in the case of bisexuality, and as he
does later with aggression.

   Let us turn now to a consideration of the ways in which the
death instinct has obscured an examination of the real psychological and social problems posed by both death and aggression.
First, by connecting aggression and death through the idea of
the return to an inorganic state, Freud clouds the fact that the
problems entailed by these two phenomena are quite different.
Death is a central psychological issue for human beings, as are
the closely related experiences of loss, separation and the grief,
anxiety and depression attendant on them. The fact that we can
think about our mortality poses a unique problem that other
animal species do not face. In addition, our special sensitivity
to loss, and the intense anxiety attendant on experiences of
separation – especially in infancy – play central roles in most
forms of psychological disturbance. All of these issues are by-
passed by the death instinct which, stated in reductionist form,
does not deal with the psychology of death at all. I will return
to the treatment of death in psychoanalytic theory shortly; let
us here consider a second way in which the death instinct version
of aggression turns attention away from important psychological
and social issues.

   By attempting to link aggression to a 'deep' biological source,
the real problems posed by human hatred, fighting, killing, rage,
guilt, sadism and masochism – in their cultural, familial, inter-
and intra-personal forms – are ignored. The death instinct version
of aggression parallels the libidinal-energy model of sexuality:
as the first avoids consideration of the psychology of anger and

fighting, the second ignores the psychology of sexual-sensual
experience. In addition, in both, the conception of instinct is
dualistic: instincts are described as originating in 'the body'
and impinging on 'the mind.' Because of this, it is impossible,
if one stays strictly within the framework of such models, to
deal with the psychology of aggression and sex. (Freud, of
course, resolves this dilemma by not remaining within the confines of his own model; with his unique style he always returns
to the important psychological issues, using his biological or
scientific-appearing terms in metaphorical ways.)

Let us consider the problem of this reductionist theory from
a somewhat different perspective. The libidinal energy model
posits a selfish, infantile pleasure principle that menaces one's
stability from sources within the body. This view, as we have
seen, is derived from the culturally-typical prejudice against
sexual pleasure and feminine qualities. The view of aggression
that posits a death instinct that exerts its inexorable force from
deep within the body, irrespective of one's life experience, is
of the same form. And, by focusing on this 'biological' source
of aggression, the theory avoids a critical examination of the
problems that arise in a society which values and rewards a
certain kind of aggression; it side-steps an examination of
aggression-as-maleness, the connections between the glorification
of the male as warrior-hero, the rewards for masculine competition
and conquest, and the destructiveness of war. In addition, the
dualist or reductionistic view of aggression as a menacing force
within, is connected to the culture's characteristic fear of
autonomy and will. Let me use the case of Schreber as an example
of this last point, and also as a way of contrasting a holistic
view of aggression with the death instinct model.

Human beings certainly behave in aggressive ways; there seems
to be something 'instinctual' going on, just as there is with the
seeking of bodily-sexual pleasure. But such instincts do not exist
outside of a social matrix which defines them, gives them form
and direction. In fact, it is our very conception of such instincts
which determines the way they are manifested: there is an
inevitable cyclical or - in many cases in the West, iatrogenic -
process at work. Schreber's father believed that any autonomy or
'willfulness' in the child was a sign of a dangerous, socially
disruptive instinct - a serious threat to adult authority - which
must be blocked, disciplined and crushed. Persons who, as
children, experience such treatment of their autonomous strivings
come, as adults, to feel the same way about them: *the instinct is
shaped by its social definition and treatment*. In other words, if
autonomous and potentially healthy aggressive strivings are
severely punished - and Schreber's case was an extreme version
of typical European practice - one comes to view such impulses
as violent and fear-related forces within oneself that must be
struggled against and repressed. One develops a personal
version of a 'death instinct' theory. The cyclical connection:
cultural conception of instinct → treatment of instinctual mani-

festations in childhood → personal paradigm → cultural paradigm, works the same as it did with sexuality. There, Freud's view of the pleasure principle as an insatiable and dangerous drive both stems from and, at the same time, reinforces beliefs in the early and severe interference with the infant's pleasure seeking activities.

When the attack on willfulness and autonomy is combined with severe sexual supression, as was often the case, and when one is prevented from expressing anger towards authorities, as was also typically the case, the stage is set for severe internal conflicts involving all these emotions. One turns rage against oneself, or against those aspects of oneself – sexuality, autonomy – involved in the childhood struggles. Schreber's severe unconscious super-ego is a classic example. Such frustrated and displaceable aggression also provides fuel for angry attacks on the 'others' – those who appear more sexually free, more autonomous, on women, on the lazy lower classes, on uncivilized foreigners, savages and primitives – who symbolize one's repressed conflicts.

In sum, the actual form of the problems posed by human aggression at any particular time and place is always inseparable from the way in which the instinct is conceptualized and treated at that time and place – from the cultural paradigm in which it is embedded. A pathological superego such as Schreber's is an iatrogenic condition, just as were the neurotic sexual lives of Freud's patients.

DEATH AND LOSS

The 'death instinct' theory of 'Beyond the Pleasure Principle' has the same sort of problems with the real issues of death and loss as it does with aggression. Like aggression in its experiential form, the importance of separations, losses and death are to be found throughout Freud's writings. And, like aggression again, these intense human concerns do not find theoretical articulation until quite late: there is a major statement in 'Mourning and Melancholia' of 1917, and a clear theoretical version in 'Inhibitions, Symptoms and Anxiety' of 1926. Prior to that, issues of death, loss, separation and anxiety are, in the theory, subordinated to the mechanics of libidinal energy. But actual deaths, losses and separations abound in the case studies, showing Freud's awareness of their importance. Let me review the evidence from the cases here and then consider why it was difficult to include death and loss in the theory.

Anna O., the first of the cases in the 'Studies on Hysteria,' develops her symptoms while nursing her dying father. It is clear that her anxiety, her collapse, and many of her specific symptoms are symbolically related to her father's illness and death. Her nervous cough appears in conjunction with his lung infection and the development of her arm paralysis – the way her arm became 'dead' – from an incident when it had 'fallen asleep'

over the back of her chair while she was sitting by his death
bed. Her sensitivity to loss is illustrated by the intensification
of her symptoms whenever Breuer leaves on vacation.[2]

The other women discussed in 'The Studies' had similar experiences with loss. Emmy von N. - the first of the cases described
by Freud- 'was one of 14 children of which she herself is the
thirteenth. Only four of them survive. . . . [She marries at
twenty-three.] After a short marriage he [the husband] died
of a stroke. . . . Since her husband's death, fourteen years
ago, she has been constantly ill [with neurosis] with varying
degrees of severity.' Thus this deeply disturbed woman suffered
through the deaths of ten of her brothers and sisters, and then
that of her husband. Her early recollections are of fright when
siblings threw dead animals at her and, at age seven, an attack
of fear when seeing a dead sister in her coffin. She experienced
other horrible losses, including seeing a cousin taken to an
insane asylum and finding her mother lying on the floor from a
stroke.

Actual death is not so clear in the case of Lucy R., though the
theme of separation and loss of love is prominent [see pp. 114-15].
The case of Katharina has already been discussed in Chapter 4.
While there were no deaths, the outcome of the family's sexual
disputes was a loss of father's attention (obviously a mixed
blessing) and a separation from him.

Elizabeth von R. is described by Freud as follows:

First the patient's father had died, then her mother had had to
undergo a serious eye-operation and soon afterwards a married
sister had succumbed to a heart-affliction of long-standing after
a confinement. In all these troubles and in all the sick-nursing
involved, the largest share had fallen to our patient (p. 135).

Death, loss, separations and the loss of love are prominent in
all the cases described in 'The Studies.' These same factors play
a prominent role in Freud's other cases as well. The Rat Man, as
we saw in Chapter 4, experienced the death of a sister in childhood, which served to connect his fears of sexual transgression
and the fear of death. Dora, as we again saw in Chapter 4, was
deprived of her mother's love and attention - due to the mother's
own severe disturbance - and continually sought love and models
in her father's world. And there, she no sooner made an attachment - to Frau K for example - than she was rejected. The Wolf
Man grew up in an aristocratic family where he was raised mainly
by servants. He was continually being left by his parents, who
were both severely disturbed - probably psychotic - so that their
capacity to relate to him, even when physically present, was no
doubt erratic. The development of anxiety and the fear of horses
in the case of Little Hans is interpreted by Freud along the well-
known lines of the Oedipus complex: that is, in terms of sexual
attraction to the mother, rivalry with the father and fear of his
castrating counter-attack. But the case is open to other interpretations, even from the evidence that Freud himself presents.
As Bowlby (1973, pp. 284-7) notes, it was primarily the mother

who threatened Hans with castration and, of perhaps even greater significance, with desertion. The parents did in fact separate shortly after the events described in the case. Finally, Schreber, whose life we examined in detail in the last chapter, suffered a massive deprivation of love from earliest infancy and this loss - or lack - was central to his pathology.

In sum, death, loss and the loss of love are striking factors in all of Freud's cases. Why, then, did it take so long for them to find expression in the general theory? There were many reasons but I wish, here, to focus on one which I consider crucial.

Death and loss are universal human experiences and, while always painful and traumatic, they do not always occasion neurotic reactions. In the prescientific age, coming to terms with death - both the thought of one's own or the actual deaths of relatives, friends and other members of one's group - was the province of religion. In primitive cultures, a death is typically the occasion for a ritual in which the members of the group mourn, dance, sing, share food and physical closeness and in other ways, both concrete and symbolic, reaffirm their connection with each other and the world of nature. (See the account of the Pygmy 'Molimo' festival in Turnbull, 1961, 1965.) Death is the ultimate separation and, more than any other, reminds us of the limits of our ego, of our ultimate smallness in the large flow of natural events. The participants in primitive rituals deal with this threat by losing themselves - their individual egos - in an ecstatic-emotional experience in which they become one with the group as the group, in turn, becomes one with its environment. Our religions are meant to serve this function and, for those who are able to believe unequivocally and to emotionally lose themselves, they may be effective. But, of course, it is difficult for many of us to remain believers of this sort in the modern world.

Lifton (1976) presents a more general discussion of this topic. He notes the threat posed by death and summarizes the principal means by which men have attempted to affirm their belief in the continuity of life in the face of this threat. These include: living on through one's children and, more broadly, through one's group; the theological conception of a life after death or, more generally, the idea of a spiritual existence beyond the death of the body; living on through nature itself, the theme of 'eternal nature'; and states of experiential transcendence such as are achieved in ecstatic rituals or with the use of certain drugs. As one can see, these modes of coping with death fall within what I have earlier termed the *human-within-nature* world view. All of them, in some sense, recognize the vulnerability of the individual human being. All involve an acceptance of our mortality and attempt to affirm the positive potential of our place in the natural world.

Another aspect of the approaches which affirm the connection with nature is their maternal, feminine or passive-receptive quality. Women, of course, are associated with birth and the nurturance of life. We all begin our lives in close connection with our mothers and the psychological separation from her heralds the onset of our

independent ego. Much of the symbolism of human-within-
nature rituals and religions involve the fusion of male and female, the losing of oneself in 'mother nature', a return to an
'egoless' state of oneness with the group, and such concrete
activities as eating, drinking and sexual stimulation that re-
arouse the sensations of early mother-infant experiences. To
put it in other terms: the rituals associated with this world
view contain a strong maternal component: they are bisexual -
Dionysian - rather than partriachal or Apollonian.

The way of civilized man contrasts with these primitive modes
of dealing with the threat of death. It takes the threat possessed
by our vulnerable place in the flow of nature as a challenge: if
we are a part of nature and subject to its death-dealing ways,
then this is a fate we must struggle against. Nature is seen as
a hostile power 'out there' - separate from our reasoning ego -
a power that we must master with ingenuity, reason, intelligence,
control and the construction of barriers - houses, cities, anti-
biotics, insecticides, or more powerful scientific theories and
advancing technology - that ward it off. This approach takes
our marvelous potential to separate ourselves from our feelings,
needs and place in the world - our genius as tool maker and
language user - and extends it to the problem of death. And,
this approach is associated with men and qualities defined as
'masculine': it is aggressive and active in contrast to loving and
passive, its images are those of warrior and hero rather than
of mother and healer.

Let me stress that the practices and beliefs associated with
each of these world views have value. The accomplishments
associated with science have done much for the advancement
of human culture. But problems arise when the man-against-
nature world view is pushed to the extreme. For with all the
achievements of our way of life, we are no less subject to
death than before. In fact, the very artifacts spawned by
modern society - armaments, cars, industrial pollutants, or the
general stress of life in crowded industrial cities - may cause
a higher proportion of deaths than the 'forces of nature' ever
did for primitive persons. Heroic immortality doesn't work, we
die in any case, with death made more painful due to the lack
of a belief system that gives it meaning. As Freud himself
remarked in a late mood of humorous despair: 'immortality
evidently means being loved by any number of anonymous
people.'[3]

Insofar as Freud's early theories were part of the man-against-
nature world view, they could not treat the problems of death
and loss outside of this framework. This is why it took so long
for him to give death and loss the central place in psychoanalytic theory that their great frequency in the clinical cases
would seem to have demanded.

To sum up: both aggression and death were treated inconsis-
tently by Freud because of the unfinished transition in world
views. One finds the same mixture of conventional and critical

assumptions and values in the exposition of these topics as
there was with sexuality and masculinity-femininity. In the
early works, aggression, death, loss and separation are discussed on an experiential level but find no place in the general
theory. When they first make their way into the theory they
remain trapped within the conventional framework as our discussion of the death instinct has shown. To move beyond this
framework is to move to a position potentially critical – in a
most profound way – of the way of life of the civilized state.
For a critical view of aggression must examine the unspoken
acceptance of male-centered values – competition, achievement,
and heroic action – while a related look at death and separation
will reveal the cost in grief and anxiety occasioned by the
lack of maternal, life-connected beliefs and rituals, as well as
the effects of disrupted and insufficient mother love.

Yet, for all of the difficulties in treating these topics in ways
consistent with the new psychoanalytic world view – for all the
persistence of old values and assumptions, all the ambivalence –
there is a steady forward movement within Freud's work. And,
in 'Civilization and its Discontents', he clears up many of the
ambiguities: in the course of this essay, one finds a remark-
able shift in theory.

WHAT DOES CAUSE CIVILIZATION'S DISCONTENTS?

'Civilization and its Discontents' is a discussion of the possibilities for human happiness and of the many difficulties that block
the path to that goal. Years of exposure to the unconscious
lives of suffering individuals, the massive destructiveness of the
First World War, the rise of fascism in Europe, his own cancer,
and the mixed reception of his genius and his creation – psychoanalysis – had all confirmed Freud's skepticism, if not down-
right pessimism, concerning civilized society. As he explores
the question of happiness he makes clear that its achievement
is a matter of the fit, or lack of fit, between human potential
or instincts and the demands of society. The possibilities for
happiness and its converse, neurotic suffering, must be understood in terms of *conflict* between these two sources; much of
the discussion of 'Civilization' explores the details of this conflict. Freud is quite persuasive in showing how, despite
scientific and technological progress, many remain unhappy.
Indeed, this is a paradox in need of a solution: why do so
many suffer in the midst of civilization's highest achievements?

As a general answer to the question of why it is so hard for
civilized human beings to be happy one can, to put it crudely,
either blame our instincts or blame society. As much of the
present book has attempted to demonstrate, the conventional
legacy within psychoanalysis arises from and perpetuates the
state's own view of itself. This is the view of human nature
and society from the perspective of the isolated intellect, from

the male or patriarchal position; it casts the blame on feminine qualities - on sexuality, pleasure, maternity, the longing for connection and oneness - and does not question or criticize existing values: the glorification of reason, the assumptions that nature, our instincts and our fellow men are enemies that we must struggle against.

The first four chapters of 'Civilization' are a continuation of this line of reasoning, a perpetuation of conventional views. Then, in two brief chapters, Freud reverses his ground, makes a major modification in his theory of instincts, detaches aggression from sexuality, gives it an independent status and, in the remaining chapters, develops a line of thought critical of the civilization he had heretofore accepted. In this new view, unhappiness is traced to aggression between men and aggression turned against the self in the form of punitive conscience (superego) and the sense of guilt. Where the first portion of 'Civilization' describes female-maternal qualities as a longing for love that is, at base, infantile, insatiable and the root cause of the perennial dissatisfaction, unhappiness and neurotic suffering of human beings, the last three chapters recast these same qualities as *Eros*. Eros is presented as the great binding force of human nature, the principal hope for happiness in the face of destructive aggression and death. In the terms I have been using, Freud makes a major shift away from the male-centered perspective, sees its assumptions and way of life in a much more critical light, and moves toward a new valuation of suppressed feminine qualities, which he terms *Eros*. It is a tribute to his genius that he was still capable of this sort of change, that his ideas were still developing at this late stage of his career (he was seventy-five when he wrote this essay). Here, in greater detail, is how the discussion in 'Civilization' develops and how it connects to the larger themes under review.

'Civilization and its Discontents' begins:

It is impossible to escape the impression that people commonly use false standards of measurement - that they seek power, success and wealth for themselves and admire them in others, and that they underestimate what is of true value in life (S.E., vol. 21, p. 64 - all further quotations are from this source).

If 'power, success and wealth' - archtypical values of the modern state - are not what is of 'true value in life,' what is? By the end of 'Civilization,' Freud's answer will be Eros, but he must first work his way through a number of skeptical arguments regarding the various manifestations of love.

He initially takes up the themes of love and human connection as they are found in religion. In 'The Future of an Illusion' of 1927 he had argued that attempts to seek happiness through religion are infantile since they are, essentially, transformations of the child's search for an all-powerful father. His friend, the novelist Romain Rolland, had suggested another source of religious feeling, something quite apart from the paternal authority and dogma of the organized church. Rolland described this as an 'oceanic' feeling and suggested that it could provide the energy for religion's many and varied forms. This oceanic feeling – which Freud describes as a sense of eternity, a feeling of 'an indissoluable bond, of being one with the external world as a whole' – could be a source of religious happiness quite apart from the infantile search for a father. Indeed, this oceanic feeling or sense of oneness may be thought of as another version of a continuity-of-life, human-within-nature theme.

Freud recognizes that the sense of connection may indicate a religious path to happiness quite different than the search for a father substitute and he begins the discussion in 'Civilization' with a skeptical examination of it. He starts by tying the oceanic feeling to the earliest stage of development. This is the stage when the infant is, indeed, connected: to his mother. Freud notes that, psychologically, the infant cannot distinguish himself from his mother, nor his ego from reality: from his perspective he and his mother are 'one.' Thus, the oceanic feeling is traced to its infantile origins. This connection, in turn, can be taken in two very different ways: one criticial of infantile desire and the other critical of social conditions that disrupt mother-infant love. That is, one can see the search for oneness through religion as but another instance of man's difficulty in renouncing his infantile pleasure seeking, as one more example of unconscious narcissism or neurotic wish fulfillment. In this view, it is our insatiable hunger for love, our greediness that, once again, is revealed to underlie a seemingly more advanced social or religious feeling. This is essentially what Freud does say about the oceanic feeling – and what he will go on to say about related feelings of love – at this point in 'Civilization.'

How might the issue have been seen differently? One could, though Freud does not, trace a line of thought as follows: since happiness is associated with an oceanic feeling of oneness – of attachment and connection – and since this feeling originates in the mother-infant bond, it follows that unhappiness, anxiety and neurosis can be traced to disruptions in this bond. In other words, there is something terribly wrong with the way the modern state has structured maternal-love and it is this that lies behind anxiety, neurosis and our 'discontents.' There is much in Freud's own work that would have supported such a line of thought – for instance the many examples of death and loss discussed in the preceding section – and the new theory of anxiety, developed in the 1926 'Inhibitions, Symptoms and Anxiety,' points in exactly this direction, for there, the infant and child's experience of separation, loss and loss of love are presented as the causes of anxiety. And anxiety is described as the signal which triggers defense, resistance and neurotic symptoms. But Freud, in the opening chapters of 'Civilization,' is not yet ready to pursue this line

of reasoning. Rather, he again finds love culpable. He does
this in two ways.

First, after giving due consideration to the oceanic feeling
as the source of religion, Freud dismisses it. It is, I think,
too feminine for him; it gives too much power to the mother.
Religion, he affirms, derives from the child's search for a
father. 'I cannot think of any need in childhood as strong as
the need for a father's protection' (p. 72). I doubt if many
psychoanalysts, or other students of human infancy, would
agree with this view today; it seems so obviously an expression
of Freud's patriarchal bias.[4]

Second, the oceanic feeling is tied to the intense state of
love and this, in turn, is viewed with skepticism.

At the height of being in love the boundary between ego and
object threatens to melt away. Against all the evidence of his
senses, a man who is in love declares that 'I' and 'you' are
one, and is prepared to behave as if it were a fact (p. 66).

In this view, love is dangerous because it disrupts the boundary
of one's ego. A footnote connects the loss of ego boundary in
the state of love to the end-of-the-world delusions of paranoia
and to other examples of loss of boundaries in severe pathological states. Though Freud had begun this discussion of love
by noting that it should not be 'stigmatized as pathological,'
when connected to psychotic delusions, it certainly becomes
suspect because of the company it keeps! The problem of disturbed ego boundaries is a complex one that demands at least
a brief attempt at clarification.

In essence Freud finds love guilty by association, the
connection being the loss of ego-boundaries in intense love and
the loss of a coherent ego in states of psychosis. As evidence,
he cites the case of Schreber. There are two problems with
this connection between love and psychosis which the detailed
analysis of Schreber in the last chapter should enable us to
see. First, while there *may* be some similarity in the two states –
and Freud presents no actual examples of ego-loss in states of
love – the affective qualities of the two are diametrically opposed.
Merging with the object of one's love is pleasurable, the loss of
ego in psychosis is intensely painful, frightening and – as 'the
end of the world' imagery suggests – experienced as death.

The second problem in Freud's attempt to connect love with
psychosis derives from the same source as his attribution of
Schreber's breakdown to the emergence of passive-feminine
libido. In both these views, love is seen as a force that can
overwhelm, if not obliterate, the ego. But, as our close consideration of Schreber's childhood and life demonstrated, his
psychosis was not brought on by too much love but by its
absence, or, more accurately, by a complex of factors that
produced an adult personality so rigid, so terrified of pleasure
and freedom, and so self-hating that love was impossible.

Freud further links love and psychosis with the terminology
of libido theory: psychosis is an example of 'narcissistic'

libidinal investment - presumably love of oneself - while love
is based on an investment of libido in others or 'objects.' As
we have repeatedly seen, the language of libido is used in
two, shifting senses which makes Freud's position on the role
of love in psychosis unclear. What is the relation between love
of self and love of others in psychosis? If one takes libido
theory literally, it seems as if there is a limited amount of
love - the 'constant quantity' of libidinal energy - so that love
of others 'depletes' love of oneself. As we will see in a moment,
Freud does seem to hold this view, at least at the level of
theory. But there is another possibility: that one turns toward
one's self as a love-object because relations with others are -
or have been in childhood - so frustrating, so anxiety provok-
ing, so bound up with feelings of rage, fear and helplessness,
that one dare not risk them. Much recent evidence concerning
the family experience of persons who become psychotic supports
this second position; it shows that these individuals do, indeed,
have intensely frustrating family experiences which make it very
difficult for them to love or trust others. [5] Like Anna O.,
Katharina, Dora and Schreber, the children in these families
are subject to intensely conflicted communications and actions.
They are singularly unloved by the others in their families
(subject to 'double-binds', pseudomutuality', mystification and
rejections) and come to internalize these experiences, feeling
hate for themselves and those who have mistreated them, along
with intense longing for human contact and an even more intense
anxiety over risking such contact.

Love as a path to happiness is given further consideration in
the second chapter of 'Civilization' where it continues to be
viewed with caution and fear. Love provides a model of intensely
pleasurable states, yet it is dangerous: 'We are never so defense-
less against suffering as when we love, never so helplessly unhappy as when we have lost our loved object or its love' (p. 82).
This is true, of course - we always risk painful loss when we
allow ourselves to love. But Freud's discussion, and the examples
he gives, imply much more than this obvious risk. Underlying
his skeptical discussion of love are the same conventional assumptions that were active in the metapsychological view of libido.
Love, like libidinal energy, is potentially disruptive. There is
a scarcity of it: in early papers this occurred as the idea of
'actual neurosis' - if you used up your sexual energy in
masturbation it sapped your strength (made you 'neurasthenic').
In the metapsychological papers of 1914-15 it is seen as the

> Antithesis between ego-libido and object-libido. The more of
> the one is employed, the more the other becomes depleted.
> The highest phase of development of which object-libido is
> capable is seen in the state of being in love, when the subject
> seems to give up his own personality in favour of an object
> cathexis; while we have the opposite condition in the paranoic's
> phantasy (or self-perception) of the 'end of the world' ('On
> Narcissism,' p. 76).

We see in these ideas a carry-over of conventional sexual taboos and views of love and the feminine, for the image of having one's ego swallowed up in love is the sort of nineteenth-century idea that arises from the same source which feared children would be overwhelmed with sexual feelings if they touched their genitals, saw adults engaged in sexual intercourse, or sucked their thumbs. That is, it is based on a *fear of love* - of losing one's ego, of being engulfed - that is not endemic to love, but arises when love, like sex, has long been infused with excessive prohibitions and taboos. Within this system of belief, love cannot even be conceptualized apart from images of loss and engulfment. Surely states of egolessness, or the fusion of self with other, occur in love relationships. But the person who is not overly anxious about love - who does not feel love and sex as threats, who does not experience intense guilt concomitant with intimacy - could enjoy such states of connection. They should not pose a threat of permanent ego loss except, again, in the individual with severe inner conflicts. Of course there is the real danger of painful loss when one loves but, as Freud himself has pointed out in other places, relationships of love are central to a meaningful life: the greater pain and loss is incurred by the person who cannot or does not risk such relationships.

To sum up so far, we have seen how Freud's discussion of love has continued to link it with frightening images of loss. If one fully gives way to love there is the danger of losing the love object. In intense states of love there is the danger of losing one's ego in a fusion with the object. Connected to these dangerous conditions are the images of loss of reason and loss of ego in psychosis. And behind all of these is the ultimate loss: death itself. Intense experiences of love and sexual involvement are pictured as death-like. To this cluster of imagined fears - love-fusion, loss of ego, loss of sanity, death - Freud opposes another cluster: tempered love (sublimated or 'aim-inhibited libido'), reason, the way of science and civilization. There is, in other words, a permissible - a less dangerous - form of love: one that is somewhat desexualized. Freud's advocacy of this reason-modulated love, along with the fears of love and loss, can be traced to the conventional valuation of reason over emotion and male qualities over the female. Within this framework, departures from reason, feelings of softness, weakness, dependence on women, the full expression of grief and mourning, or almost any intense experience of emotion, are viewed as threats to one's precariously defended masculine integrity. In other words, the fear of loss - of ego, of love object, of sanity - is connected to man's fear of women and the feminine. [6]

The fear of love and its connection with death can be understood when we realize that Freud, like most members of his society, was exposed to a scarcity of love in infancy and childhood. And this experience led to ambivalence towards love

itself and the 'objects' of love - women and mothers. If one is
subject to prolonged deprivation of a normal human desire or
activity, it often acquires a greatly intensified value. Thus,
persons who are starving become obsessed with elaborate
gastronomical fantasies. The 'sexual' nature of curiosity and
looking, as another example, was greatly enhanced, if not
created, by the secrecy surrounding sexual functions and the
sight of the human body characteristic of Freud's time. Sexuality *is* intrinsically interesting because of the bodily-pleasurable
feelings involved, but the *sexualization* of curiosity is intensified by the extensive cover-up; children will be strongly driven
to look at the exciting mysteries that are so valued (both
positively and negatively) that they are surrounded by great
numbers of garments, locked doors and taboos.

The sexualization of curiosity exemplifies a more pervasive conflict: powerful-threatening desires aroused by deprivation of
human contact, love and sensual pleasure in the infancy and
childhood of most persons in Freud's society. It was common for
them to be pushed away from physical contact with adults and
to be weaned early. They were then threatened or punished for
those transitional actions (thumb-sucking, masturbation and
sexual play) with which young children bridge the gap from
mother's love to increasing independence. They were, in many
ways, expected to renounce the sensual-pleasurable experiences
associated with love at an extremely early age and to behave
like 'little men' and 'little women.' Thus, like victims of starva-
tion, they came to adult love from a background of deprivation,
anxiety, rage and guilt; a background conducive to fantasies
which exaggerate the power of the deprived experience. I think
the image of being swallowed up in love - of losing one's ego
in the other - is just such a fantasy. *It is the wonderful-
terrifying vision of a love-starved society.* The more deprived
in early life, the more intense is this conflict likely to be,
which fits with observations of severely disturbed persons whose
fear of the love they long for is often expressed in fantasies
of engulfment and loss of ego or self.

Freud's skeptical treatment of love in the initial chapters of
'Civilization' reflects the continuing influence of conventional,
male-centered values, values which had so much influence
throughout his theories. In his view of the oedipal conflict, for
example, it is the father's power as rival and castrator that is
the prime source of anxiety, rather than the loss of mother's
love and care. In 'Totem and Taboo' (1913), civilization itself
is pictured as originating out of a battle between the primeval
father and the band of son-brothers. Freud imagines a pre-
civilized state in which a tyrannical father ruled over the sons,
hoarding the women to himself. The brothers must kill him to
get their share, but their crime is the origin of guilt and self-
control and, hence, the beginnings of the rule of law and
civilization. While this fantasy captures an aspect of the conflicts of civilization, one is struck by what it leaves out. For

where are mothers, love, child care, and family ties in all
this? How did the sons and brothers - or the primeval father
himself for that matter - ever reach adulthood? Who nursed and
cared for them? The image of 'Totem and Taboo' seems characteristic of western fantasies that neglect the role of women and
repress man's feminine side, that try to derive civilization's
achievements from the clash of male aggression, rivalry and
power.

Where 'Totem and Taboo' located the origins of guilt, conscience and civilized rule in the son's overthrow of the father,
other works depicted women as ethically inferior, with 'weak
super-egos' and less capacity for guilt. Thus, in the 1915
'Observations on Transference Love' Freud speaks of

women of elemental passionateness who tolerate no surrogates.
They are children of nature who refuse to accept the
psychical in place of the material, who, in the poet's
words, are accessible only to 'The logic of soup, with
dumplings for arguments'. With such people one has the choice
between returning their love or else bringing down upon oneself the full enmity of a woman scorned (pp. 166-7).

Few would deny that there are *people* (men and women) who
act this way, but Freud singles out women. The image of 'women
of an elemental passionateness' reminds us of the earlier example
of the 'love-object' that is capable of swallowing up the man's
ego. The call of Circe and the Sirens is audible here; the woman
as seductress or temptress, unable to control her passion and
luring the male to a state of dissolution. To the clinically
experienced, this sounds like the projection of a fantasy, a
fantasy about women from the male unconscious.

Yet, while this general view of women, sexuality, motherhood
and love is a persistent and dominant theme throughout Freud's
writings, it undergoes a complete reversal in the final four
chapters of 'Civilization and its Discontents.' In Chapter 4,
preparatory to this reversal, he is again considering love as a
potential path toward human happiness. Here is a crucial
passage:

Women soon come into opposition to civilization and display
their retarding and restraining influence - those very women
who, in the beginning, laid the foundations of civilization by
the claims of their love. Women represent the interests of the
family and of sexual life. The work of civilization has become
increasingly the business of men, it confronts them with ever
more difficult tasks and compels them to carry out instinctual
sublimations of which women are little capable. Since a man
does not have unlimited quantities of psychichal energy at
his disposal, he has to accomplish his tasks by making an
expedient distribution of his libido. What he employs for
cultural aims he to a great extent withdraws from women
and sexual life. His constant association with men, and his
dependence on his relations with them, even estrange him
from his duties as a husband and father. Thus, the woman

finds herself forced into the background by the claims of
civilization and she adopts a hostile attitude towards it
(pp. 103-4).

This passage is interesting in several ways. Freud continues
to view women as opposed to civilization and as aligned with
sexuality and love, but adds an emphasis on their commitment
to 'the family.' While he places men at the center of civilized
business, much of the discussion in the essay up to this point
has been critical of just what that business is. Crucial, of
course, are the examples one supplies for the conflicting interests alluded to in the quoted passage. If one thinks of the
'work of civilization' as science and art, then women's opposition –
their 'retarding and restraining influence' in favor of love –
seems a form of infantile selfishness. But if one thinks of the
work of civilization as warfare, as the conquest and subjugation
of foreign peoples, as sending young children into coal mines
and factories where they are worked into a state of ill-health
and early death, then women's opposition – their 'restraining
influence' – appears in quite a different light. It is the mother's
perennial cry against the state's conscription of her son, her
protest against his use as a cog in the machinery of war or
industry. Recall that Freud wrote 'Civilization' in 1930, in
Europe, after the immense and senseless slaughter of the First
World War, on the threshold of the new Nazi barbarism. His
views on love, civilization and the causes of unhappiness are
about to undergo a radical shift; one can almost feel him
struggle to a new position in the writing of this essay.

Chapter 5 moves from an emphasis on the roles of love and
sexuality in human unhappiness to an increasing recognition of
the force of aggression. In his skeptical discussion of the
commandment 'love thy neighbor as thyself,' Freud brings forth
many heartfelt examples of man's hostility to his fellow man. By
Chapter 6 he takes a clear position: aggression has a primary
instinctual status, it is a motive force separate from sexuality
and libido, and one with great power and importance. Here
is how he puts it;

> I know that in sadism and masochism we have always seen
> before us manifestations of the destructive instinct . . .
> strongly allayed with erotism; but I can no longer understand
> how we can have overlooked the ubiquity of non-erotic aggres-
> sivity and destructiveness and can have failed to give it its
> due place in our interpretation of life (p. 119).

And, at the conclusion of Chapter 6:

> In all that follows, I adopt the standpoint, therefore, that
> the inclination to aggression is an original, self-subsisting
> instinctual disposition in man, and I return to my view that
> it constitutes the greatest impediment to civilization. . . . I
> may now add that civilization is a process in the service of
> Eros, whose purpose is to combine single human individuals,
> and after that families, then races, peoples and nations, into
> one great unity, the unity of mankind (p. 122).

He goes on to elaborate the image of civilization as a struggle
between Eros and destructiveness, between the forces of love
and those of aggression.

Several things should be emphasized about this shift in
Freud's thought. First, we see a clear abandonment of libido
or sexuality as the single instinct to which all others were
reduced. While aggression, anger, hostility and related forces
found a place in earlier writings, the theoretical treatment
always linked them with sexuality, usually with the terminology
of 'sadism' and 'masochism.' Freud breaks that linkage in the
passage quoted above. There are certainly instances of sexualized-
hatred and aggressivized-sexuality, but aggression and the
problem it poses for human social life cannot be reduced to a
unitary sexual instinct. In the present terms, the masculine-
evil, as in warfare, cannot be derived from the feminine.

In addition to abandoning the sexual reductionism of libido
theory, Freud has made a still larger shift. Where before it
was sexuality, with its unceasing hunger for gratification,
that stood in opposition to civilization and so was the basic
source of human unhappiness, it is now aggression. And this
same sexuality – clothed in its abstract name of Eros to be sure –
is seen as the great pro-civilization force. In the terms I have
been using, Freud has struggled free from the male-centered
perspective and reached a new vantage point from which all
appears different. If we take Eros as a referent for mother-
love, for suppressed femininity, for sexuality, for the female-
maternal principal – and I think Freud's use is such that this
is precisely how we should take it – we see that depreciated
feminine qualities have received a new valuation. And, if we
equate what he is now calling the aggressive or destructive
instinct with masculine qualities, with the father principle, with
the drive for power and domination – and I think this is consistent with his usage – it is apparent that these previously
extolled male qualities are now seen in a much more critical
light. He now more clearly questions the values of the civilization, the science and the achievements that he had been
committed to for so long. One can see how this shift in viewpoint in 'Civilization' expands the conception of human nature
by viewing both male and female qualities in terms of their
productive and destructive potentials.

'Civilization' began by questioning the 'false standards' of
society – 'power, success and wealth' – and by searching for
what is 'of true value in life.' That stated the problem on a
descriptive level. After working through the various skeptical
arguments concerning love and human connection, Freud found
a way of treating the problem theoretically: with the introduction of an aggressive instinct separate from sexuality – and
associated with masculine qualities – he is able to view the
conflicts of civilization in terms of a broader perspective, one
in which he can more directly discuss the destructive effects
of unbalanced masculine aggressiveness.

The final two chapters of 'Civilization' continue to open new possibilities. In a summary fashion this is what Freud says. Aggression is the chief cause of human unhappiness, both in the obvious form of conflict between persons and in the more subtle form of 'conscience.' In developing this second, crucial point, Freud relies on the theory of identification, introduced in 'Mourning and Melancholia' and elaborated in 'The Ego and the Id' (see the discussion in the chapter on bisexuality). In that theory, the child's emotionally conflicted relationships with the parents are resolved by an identification with them in which what was an *external* conflict - between misbehaving child and critical or punitive parent - becomes an *internal* conflict between one part of the person and the other. This is the well-known account in which the conscience or superego develops as the internal voice of parental criticism and control. While this basic theory was present in earlier works, 'Civilization' sharpens the focus on the primary role of aggression; the self-punishing superego is aggression turned on the self.

'Conscience' is ready to put into action against the ego the same harsh aggressiveness that the ego would have liked to satisfy upon other, extraneous individuals (p. 122).

In his account of the origins of the ego's aggressiveness toward others, Freud stresses the frustrations of pleasurable activities, loss of love and the fears or 'social anxiety' engendered by parental threats. These conditions make it difficult for the child to express his anger and foster an internalization in which 'the aggressiveness of conscience keeps up the aggressiveness of the authority' (p. 128).

Sexuality is introduced into the discussion but in a very different way than in earlier views:

If we suppose, that is, that the prevention of an erotic satisfaction calls up a piece of aggressiveness against the person who has interfered with the satisfaction; and that this aggressiveness has itself to be suppressed in turn. But if this is so, it is after all only the aggressiveness which is transformed into a sense of guilt by being suppressed and made over to the superego (p. 128).

In other words, the punitive superego and sense of guilt are fueled primarily by aggression; the discontents of civilization are not so much a matter of an insatiable pleasure principle as of the excessive *oppression of sexuality* by internalized aggression.

The final sections of 'Civilization' raise further questions about the harsh and impossible demands of society - demands and frustrations that create aggression which, in turn, feeds into conscience, the sense of guilt and neurotic suffering. Freud's conclusion is very clear: in discussing the course of the essay he states:

It corresponds faithfully to my intention to represent the sense of guilt as the most important problem in the development of civilization and to show that the price we pay for our advance in civilization is a loss of happiness through the heightening of the sense of guilt (p. 134).

Thus, it is civilization itself that causes the discontents of civilized citizens. Anxiety, neurotic suffering, and guilt are the price that is paid for the accomplishments, the benefits, the triumphs of modern society. These painful conditions do not result from human instincts per se, but from the particular way in which such instinctual forces as aggression and sexuality are channeled and oppressed in the modern world. This view of the consequences of civilized life seems to me quintessentially psychoanalytic. Freud has found a way of analyzing his society from a position of neutrality somewhere 'outside' it, just as he analyzed his patients. It is an instance of what I earlier termed the examination of a paradigm from a metaparadigmatic position. This mode of analysis, in which Freud has freed himself from conventional values, shows how the final chapters of 'Civilization' are a completion of the unfinished journey. This is apparent, especially in the final chapter, where his discussion of sexuality and aggression, of the interpersonal and social origins of anxiety and guilt, and the reappraisal of male and female qualities as aggression and Eros, are all carried forth from a position at odds with conventional assumptions, from a position clearly within the new psychoanalytic world view.

A CONCLUDING NOTE

On a deep level, the problems in creating and maintaining a psychoanalytic world view persist for all who follow the path that Freud opened. The journey - the transition in perspectives - will never be completed. If we have managed to move beyond some of the conventional values that were Freud's starting place, we are caught up in new versions that arise from our current social framework. To be engaged in psychoanalytic work is to be exposed to the unconscious of oneself and others. And this exposure confronts one with the price in conflict, anxiety, guilt, alienation and pain that is paid for the outward success, benefits and accomplishments of our society. What is one to do with the heretical knowledge gained in this way?

If Freud, the most inventive and insightful psychological genius of the century, had difficulty in fully freeing himself from the biases of his society, what chance do we have in transcending ours? We have his work - and that of the many who have elaborated, expanded and modified it - to build on, of course. And we live in a different age, one presumably more open-minded, democratic and understanding. But is it so different? How much of what seems new and modern to us is really different from the world that Freud knew? When one looks past surface changes in technology and social relations, at such underlying dimensions as the relative valuation of male and female qualities, one wonders at the depth of change. It may be true that psychoanalysis itself, and the many related forms of therapy, reflect some larger change in social consciousness. There seems to be a greater awareness of the unconscious, of the importance of subjectivity, intuition and emotional experience, changes that are reflected in modern fiction, drama and art. Perhaps, of even greater importance, there have been major shifts in the treatment of children, with more recognition of the infant's need for love and maternal care, and a diminution of punitive discipline.

Yet, for all these changes, the dominant value system in the West retains many of its traditional qualities: the life of reason and objectivity, of work and control remain powerful ideals. Do not many still seek 'power, success and wealth for themselves and admire them in others, and . . . underestimate what is of true value of life'? Things appear to change yet they stay the same. And it is an awareness of the strength of conventional values that I would urge on all who work within the general framework of psychoanalysis, an awareness of how easy it is for old ideas and assumptions to masquerade as 'new' or 'modern' theory, therapy or social criticism. We should be guided by the spirit embodied in Freud's life and work and try to view both old and new, both the conventional and revolutionary, with equal understanding. Experience should make us cautious of fixed truths, of answers and of certainty. It must be our task to question, to look beneath the surface, to view familiar events from yet another perspective, in short, to psychoanalyze.

NOTES

CHAPTER 1 ON READING FREUD

1 A number of papers and books treat this issue; Pribram and Gill (1976) is perhaps the most detailed. See also: Amacher (1965); Holt (1965); and Gill and Holtzman (1976).

CHAPTER 2 PERSPECTIVES OLD AND NEW

1 I will use the terms 'perspective' and 'world view' to carry the discussion throughout most of the text. The closely related 'schema' and 'paradigm' have more specific definitions, the first in Piaget's theory of cognitive development and the second in Kuhn's analysis of physical science, though both are used in broader ways by other authors. The central meaning of all these concepts - as well as 'guiding image', the phrase preferred by Lifton (1976) and 'set', from an older tradition in the psychology of perception - overlap. They are ways of referring to the same general phenomena.

2 For a full discussion and much supporting evidence on hunter-gatherer cultures, see 'Man the Hunter' (1968), a collection of papers edited by Lee and DeVore. A detailed picture of life among the !Kung may be gleaned from Marshall (1976) and Lee and DeVore (1976). My discussion of feeding and discipline is drawn from these sources and from DeVore and Konner (1974) and Konner (1972).

3 This discussion of feeding and discipline in seventeenth-century France is based on David Hunt's excellent study, 'Parents and Children in History' (1970) and on Marvick (1974).

4 It seems impossible to discuss the treatment of masculinity and femininity today without, in the process, using words that carry a burden of traditional prejudice. I see no way around this problem so, rather than introducing qualifications each time these words are used, let me say here that I mean to refer to a set of characteristics traditionally associated with masculinity (aggression, competitiveness, hardness) and femininity (maternal love, softness, emotionality) without endorsing the conventional belief that these qualities exist only in men or in women. Nor should the use of these terms be taken to mean that these sex-role qualities are best kept segregated, that there is something pathological or abnormal about aggressive women or men with strong maternal feelings, for example. Quite the contrary, the thrust of my analysis will show that Freud's work provides the basis for a critique of the conventional overvaluation of masculine qualities as well as a critique of attempts at a rigid segregation of sex-role qualities.

5 The historian Gordon R. Taylor (1954, 1958) traces the cyclic patterning of what he calls 'patrist' and 'matrist' religious value systems through Western civilization. The patrist - similar to what I call the man-against-nature world view - is associated with a male deity, authoritarian political and religious structures, the repression of emotion and playfulness, and a fear of homosexuality. Matrist religions - related to what I call the human-within-nature world view - are associated with mother deities, equalitarian social organization, the positive evaluation of passion, and a fear of incest. Taylor's analysis is valuable in showing how Western civilization is not simply a monolithic patriarchal culture, but one which has alternated between periods of patrist and matrist influence. It is also clear from his account how patrist groups repress and dominate the matrist and how, in the last few hundred years certainly, they have

maintained political and social control.
6   Quoted in Shakow and Rapaport -The Influence of Freud on American Psychology- (1964), p. 34.

CHAPTER 3   PSYCHOANALYSIS IS *NOT* SCIENCE

1   For a discussion of this issue in the physical sciences see Polanyi (1958, 1966); in academic psychology see Bakan (1967), Chein (1972), and Koch (1959); and in psychoanalysis Fingarette (1963), Lifton (1976), and Ricoeur (1970).
2   Cogent critical analyses of the metapsychology may be found in the papers of Robert Holt (1965, 1967, 1976), and in Nathan Leites's scathing 'The New Ego' (1971). See also Yankelovich and Barrett's 'Ego and Instinct' (1970); Roy Schafer's 'A New Language for Psychoanalysis' (1976); and 'Psychology versus metapsychology' (1976), a volume edited by Gill and Holtzman. It is interesting that many of these critics were former students or collaborators of Rapaport or felt themselves within the closely related Hartmann school of ego psychology, but in their more recent writings have worked their way beyond these earlier commitments. For example, Merton Gill presents a strong argument against the metapsychology in the 1976 volume and also in the book he coauthored with Karl Pribram (Pribram and Gill, 1976). That book began as an attempt to use Freud's 'Project for a Scientific Psychology' as the basis for an integration of psychoanalytic theory with modern neurophysiology, yet, in the later sections, Gill changes his position and argues against the appropriateness of such an integration. A related change can be observed in the work of Roy Schafer, whose current efforts (1976) to formulate psychoanalysis in an 'action language' represent a major shift away from his earlier approach (1968) which was more within the metapsychological fold.
     In addition to efforts like Rapaport's, much of what is known as 'Ego Psychology' - particularly the work of Heinz Hartmann and his collaborators - became entwined with the mechanistic metapsychology. This is somewhat of a paradox since the main thrust of ego psychology was an attempt to make a legitimate theoretical space for those phenomena - the ego, conscious experience, directed action - that could not be adequately subsumed in the older 'drive psychology' associated with the metapsychology. Yet Hartmann's reluctance to part with the metapsychology and his attempts to tie psychoanalytic psychology to biology kept this version of ego psychology in the same conflicted mixture of assumptions as the older theory he was attempting to remedy. Erik Erikson's version of ego psychology is largely free of those problems, yet many psychoanalysts - even those who value his work highly as a clinician - don't think of it as 'really' theory, since it does not have the form or appearance of science. The Hartmann style of ego psychology was useful in drawing attention to, and legitimizing interest in, the so-called non-conflictual spheres of the ego. But beyond this - when one examines it as a general theory - it seems as empty as Rapaport's efforts.
3   This general way of viewing psychoanalytic theory comes from, and is supported by, the work of a number of recent writers. George Klein (see 'Psychoanalytic Theory: An Exploration of Essentials,' 1976), whose ideas we have just been discussing, makes a powerful case for the clinical theory stated in an experimential language. Robert Lifton's 'The Life of the Self' (1976) takes a related stand with its empahsis on the psychological processes of formation and transformation. See also Yankelovich and Barrett's 'Ego and Instinct' (1970), which stresses the existential as opposed to the mechanistic core of psychoanalysis; Roy Schafer's 'A New Language for Psychoanalysis' (1976), which argues for a theory stated in a language of human action; Paul Ricoeur's 'Freud and Philosophy: An Essay on Interpretation' (1970), which argues that psychoanalysis deals with the interpretation of meaning and that this sets it apart from the natural sciences; and, if I understand them correctly - and who ever

does? - the work of the contemporary French school that includes Lacan
(see Wilden, 1968) and Laplanche (1976). Also relevant is the work of
Jane Loevinger (1966); R. D. Laing (1960, 1967); and Charles Rycroft
(1967).

4   Examples of attempts to integrate information and psychoanalytic theories
may be found in Colby (1955); Rubinstein (1967); Peterfreund (1971);
and, most recently, Rosenblatt and Thickstun (1977). Pribram attempts
to show how Freud's 'Project' is consistent with modern neurology in the
book coauthored with Gill (1976). John Bowlby's model of mother-infant
attachment uses a mixture of information, ethological and general systems
theories (1969, 1973). And an early paper of mine (Breger, 1967), uses
information concepts to recast psychoanalytic dream theory.

5   While psychoanalytic subject matter is best defined by what occurs in
the analytic situation, it need not be restricted to that situation. Freud
himself, and many after him, have extended the reach of analytic insights to literature, history, anthropology, religion, child development,
and the study of civilization. Space does not permit a discussion of the
many useful modes of application, nor of the difficulties and dangers in
these various extensions of psychoanalysis. As just one example I would
recommend Meredith Skura's 'The Critic and the Psychoanalyst: Literary
Uses of the Psychoanalytic Process,' a very sophisticated treatment of
the application of psychoanalysis to literature, and a work whose point
of view overlaps with that developed here.

CHAPTER 4   THE THEORY OF SEXUALITY

1   The idea that the psychoanalytic version of sexuality exists in two forms
should be distinguished from the position that George Klein takes in his
chapter, 'Freud's two theories of sexuality' (originally published in my
book, 'Clinical-Cognitive Psychology,' 1969; it is reprinted in Gill and
Holtzman, 1976, and appears as Chapter 3 in Klein, 1976). Klein dis-
tinguishes the clinical theory of sexuality from the metapsychological
version. The clinical theory deals with the personal record of sensual
experiences, their development over life, and their connection with
anxiety and interpersonal conflict. The metapsychology, on the other
hand, is an attempt to describe human sexual experience in a language
of force, mechanism, energy and discharge, taken over from nineteenth-
century physics and neurology. Klein argues - as have Holt, Schafer
and a number of others - that the metapsychological version is anachronistic, invalid, and that it detracts from the real insights of psychoanalysis, which are better expressed in a language of human experience
and action. I am in agreement with this position, as far as it goes, and
have attempted to incorporate it, and related critical analyses of the
metapsychology, into the present book. But these analyses do not deal
with the larger differences in world view, nor with those controversial
social and political factors revolving around male and female roles, or
the work-pleasure dialectic, that are under consideration here. The two
contradictory trends under discussion cannot be aligned with Klein's
clinical theory-metapsychology distinction. The unresolved ambivalence -
the conflict between conventional and critical perspectives - is manifested
in Freud's conceptualization of cases, in discussions of psychoanalytic
therapy and in the more general or abstract statements of theory. In
other words, the conflict in world views cuts across *both* of what Klein
terms 'Freud's two theories of sexuality.'

2   As Heinz Kohut makes clear in 'The Restoration of the Self' (1977),
neuroses and other forms of psychological pathology are never a matter
of 'traumas' like a single seduction, but derive from the disturbed and
disturbing matrix of parent-child relations. As he puts it:

    But clinical experience tells us that in the great majority of cases it
    is the specific pathogenic personality of the parent(s) and specific
    pathogenic features of the atmosphere in which the child grows up
    that account for the maldevelopments, fixations and unsolvable inner

conflicts characterizing the adult personality. Stated in the obverse:
the gross events of childhood that appear to be the cause of the
later disturbances will often turn out to be no more than crystalliza-
tion points for intermediate memory systems, which if pursued further,
lead to truly basic insights about the genesis of the disturbance.
Behind the seeming importance of a child's sexual overstimulation and
conflicts with regard to his observations of parental sexual intercourse, for example, often lies the much more important absence of
the parent's empathic responses to the child's need to be mirrored
and to find a target for his idealization. It is, in other words, deprivation in the area of the sustaining matrix of empathy, not the
pressure of the child's curiosity (which is not pathogenic) that, via
depression and other forms of self-pathology, leads him to an excessive (pathological and pathogenic) involvement with the sexual life of
his parents (pp. 187-8).

Part of the current popularity of Kohut's work derives from the way
he is able to present, in language that psychoanalysts are comfortable
with, the basic model which views symptoms, neurosis and character
structure as symbolically transformed outcomes of a whole range of childhood experiences - experiences that are not confined to a single trauma,
nor to sexuality. Every competent therapist knows this from his clinical
work, of course, yet Kohut's current restatement of it is appealing because it once more moves psychoanalytic theory toward its appropriate
critical perspective in response to the inevitable drift to conventionality.

3   Contrast, in this regard, Chapter 6 with Chapter 7 of 'The Interpretation
of Dreams,' the first an extensive treatment of forms of symbolic transformation and the second a return to the reductive neuropsychology of
'The Project.'

4   See Holt (1976) for a summary of the failure of the metapsychology as a
neuropsychology, a topic dealt with by many other authors, and, also,
for an excellent review of its failure as a theory of sexuality. Very
briefly, Holt reviews evidence from many sources - physiological, ethological and psychological, human and nonhuman - which all converge on
the conclusion that a drive discharge (or tension buildup-tension discharge) theory of sexual motivation does not fit the facts. Such a theory
is not valid for hunger or thirst either; about all it comes close to explaining is urination.

5   Roy Schafer in his 'A New Language for Psychoanalysis' (1976) presents
the most detailed account and critique of the mixture of the human and
the mechanical in psychoanalytic theorizing. His basic position, a valid
one in my view, is that psychoanalysis is a human-psychological endeavor -
albeit one of a very special kind - and that this fact should be reflected
in its language. Schafer's own prescription is that psychoanalysts purge
the mixtures and inconsistencies from their discourse and confine themselves to a language of 'persons' and 'actions'. He presents numerous
examples to show that this is what psychoanalytic statements are really
about, in any case, and that the other terms and models simply obscure
this fact. While I don't think it likely that his specific prescriptions
will be widely adopted - old ways of thinking and talking seem hard to
part with - his general analysis is consistent with that of a number of
others; it is part of a growing recognition that the mechanistic, reductionistic, and scientistic models and terms in Freud's theories are remnants of old allegiances; that what is unique, new and central in his
work is often described in a language that uses these old terms in new
ways.

6   I believe that an understanding of the mixture of perspectives in this
sphere of psychoanalytic theory will help clarify the endless debates
between those - radical feminists, for example - who see Freud as the
embodiment of male chauvinism and those who see him as a champion of
the liberation of women. He is both, though the creative surge of psychoanalytic thought has, for the most part, been liberating. It is psycho-

analytic theory, or modifications of it, that explains such crucial topics as psychological bisexuality, unconscious femininity in men and masculinity in women, and all the complexities of sex-role identifications, rivalries, conflicts and defenses. Even those such as Karen Horney, who broke with the orthodox analytic movement over theoretical differences concerning women, continued to present explanations that fit within the larger psychoanalytic frame.

A good source of classic and modern papers is Miller's 'Psychoanalysis and Women' (1973). Juliet Mitchell's 'Psychoanalysis and Feminism' (1974) compares Freud's theories with those of the so-called radical psychoanalysts (Reich and Laing) and with radical feminists. She criticizes the superficiality of most of these later writers, when contrasted with the depth and subtlety of Freud, a position I share, though not for the same reasons. Jean Baker Miller's 'Toward a New Psychology of Women' (1976) presents a well-balanced discussion of these issues from what I would call a criticial psychoanalytic perspective. She is particularly illuminating on the topic of 'feminine' qualities in the broadest sense. Robert Stoller's recent work (1975, 1979) shows how one can remain a psychoanalyst while pursuing theory that is free of male-centered bias. Stoller is particularly clear on the way in which one's primary sense of masculinity and femininity develops and how it becomes enmeshed in unconscious conflict.

7   Anna O. was, in reality, Bertha Pappenheim (see Freeman, 1972, for an interesting account of her later life). She recovered from her breakdown and became a pioneer social worker who devoted the remainder of her life to helping young women who had been abandoned or exploited in various ways. She never married and her anger toward men, and a generally self-controlled manner, remained characteristic of her into old age.

A person displaying the symptoms of the young Anna would probably be labeled psychotic or schizophrenic by contemporary diagnostic standards. In fact, many of the hysterics in 'The Studies' - as well as Dora, whose case will be examined shortly - show fairly severe forms of disturbance, if not psychotic than what would now be termed 'borderline.' I mention this to counter the frequently-expressed belief that 'in the old days' Freud and his contemporaries worked with 'classical hysterics' whose dynamics were centered around the Oedipus complex, but that we 'don't see very many patients like that anymore.' A close look at Freud's cases shows that he didn't see very many such patients either. Anna O. is certainly not a classical hysteric with an unresolved Oedipus complex, nor is Dora.

8   The machinations of Dora's father and the K's is quite similar to the actions of the psychosis-producing families described in the research of Laing and Easterson (1964). Henry (1971) and others (see Bateson et al.. 1956: Laing. 1969: and Lidz. 1963). There is some interesting follow-up information on Dora in a report by the psychoanalyst Felix Deutsch (1957) though he seems unperceptive and unsympathetic to her. She consults Deutsch in her early forties, still symptom-ridden, anxious and acting out her revenge on men, with her husband as principal target. Her complaints make clear that her mother's exaggerated cleanliness and annoying washing compulsions not only made her an unattractive female model in the eyes of her young daughter, but deprived Dora of maternal love as well. Thus her mother, responding in her disturbed way to her position as a woman, deprives a daughter of love, affection and a desirable model, all factors that - together with her complex exploitation by her father and the K's - led to her lifelong anger and unhappiness.

CHAPTER 5 BISEXUALITY, AUTONOMY AND AUTHORITY: THE CASE OF SCHREBER

1   Maternity and aggression are not the only primary differences between the sexes, of course. And, even with respect to these two dimensions, there is a good deal of controversy over what is universal, what

is necessary in some biologically or socially adaptive sense, and what
is peculiar to the West, to nineteenth-century Europe, or to contemporary Emerica. See Miller (17976) for a general discussion of this issue.
Maccoby and Jacklin (1974) present a comprehensive review of research
on male-female differences.

2   A much more detailed discussion of the processes by which boys and
girls acquire their sexual identity, along with a critical examination of
Freud's ideas in this area - including his concept of bisexuality - is
provided by Robert Stoller (1968, 1972). The reader is referred to
Stoller's careful analysis for a full exploration of these issues; here I
would just note several points. First, one's basic sense of maleness or
femaleness - what Stoller terms 'core gender identity' - is acquired very
early: in the first two or three years. Acquisition of the sorts of bisexual conflicts I have been discussing come later; they represent, essentially, a filling in of what it *means* to be male or female. Second, while
biological sex is important, there is no 'biological bedrock,' as Freud
thought, that explains such psychological conflicts as penis envy in girls
or fear of femininity (masculine protest) in boys. Early interpersonal
experiences are of much greater power and, since almost all infants begin
with an attachment to their mother, we may all be said to start with a
feminine imprint. Finally, Stoller's review of modern biological evidence,
including rare biological-sexual anomalies which provide the bases for
'natural experiments,' as well as cases in which parents raise their
biologically normal children in the wrong sexual direction, all point to
the great importance of social experience - and particularly early
experience with the mother. As Stoller puts it:

> The effects of these biological systems, organized prenatally in a
> masculine or feminine direction, are almost always . . . too gentle in
> humans to withstand the more powerful forces of environment in human
> development, the first and most profound of which is mothering (1972,
> p. 211).

3   As an example of Freud's use of his critical model of sexual identity conflict, see his report, 'The Psychogenesis of a Case of Homosexuality in
a Woman' (1920b). The case concerns a young woman who develops a
homosexual passion for a 'society lady' ten years her senior. The essence
of Freud's analysis of her homosexuality is as follows: her own mother
rejected her, favored her brothers and was jealous of any potential
closeness between the girl and her father. When she was sixteen, her
mother gave birth to yet another brother, intensifying her feelings of
rivalry and rejection. She turned away from her mother, and from an
identification with her as a woman, and adopted a homosexual orientation. The older 'society lady,' with whom she became romantically
obsessed, was both a love object and a substitute mother figure. Her
actions in relation to this woman, and her attempt to assume a male
identity, arose from the intense interpersonal conflicts within her family,
her painful rejection in favor of male siblings, her mother's own rivalry
for the father and her desperate search for acceptance and love. A
comparison of Freud's discussion of this young woman with his discussion
of Dora, whose dynamics were similar, shows how far his thinking had
moved from its earlier form. His explanation in the present case is
entirely in terms of the effects of intense interpersonal conflicts and
their internal representations. In other words, the young woman's bisexual conflicts are seen as an expression of the difficulties she experienced in identifying with her mother due to their rivalry and the
culturally-typical valuation of males (her brothers) and depreciation
of women.

4   Schreber's book was translated into English in 1955 by Macalpine and
Hunter as 'Memoirs of My Mental Illness,' and I will refer to it hereafter
as the 'Memoirs.'

5   In its way, the theory outlined in the 'Memoirs' is like Freud's metapsychology, in which certain terms and ideas from physical science and

neurology are used as symbols for human feelings and experiences. Is Schreber's theory psychotic and Freud's metapsychology - with its mythical 'libidinal energies,' 'cathecting objects,' 'deflecting from its aims,' 'discharging' in sex or being 'sublimated' - scientific? The reader must decide for himself; in my own view, the two theories may be more alike than not.

6   Niederland's papers, along with those of several other psychoanalysts, are collected in 'The Schreber Case' (Niederland, 1974). Morton Schatzman, a psychiatrist influenced by R. D. Laing, presents an analysis of the interrelationship of father and son from a different perspective in his book, 'Soul Murder: Persecution in the Family' (1973). See also the symposium edited by Kitay (1963). I will draw on all these sources in the discussion to follow.

7   The methods advocated by Schreber's father may strike the contemporary reader as extremely harsh, if not sadistic, and the question may be raised as to whether they are at all typical of nineteenth-century European child-rearing. A good deal of evidence supports the view that Doctor Schreber - if himself a bit thorough - expressed views of childhood and discipline that were typical of the period. He was a widely revered authority whose books sold extremely well. Beyond this, there is evidence, recently reported by a number of historians, concerning the treatment - or perhaps one should say mistreatment - of children in past centuries of western civilization. De Mause (1974a) presents a detailed, if somewhat gruesomely overdone, review of evidence which points to much child abuse, deprivation and failure to understand the needs of young children. Even those who are skeptical of the picture De Mause paints (see Stone, 1974 for a critical review), are in essential agreement that large numbers of infants and children suffered deprivation of maternal care as well as harsh and punitive discipline in the recent past. Additional sources include Abt-Garrison (1965); Despert (1965); Hunt (1970); Wishy (1968); other chapters in the 1974 volume edited by De Mause (1974b) and issues of 'The History of Childhood Quarterly.'

8   Schreber's self-therapy is a more tumultuous version of similar processes seen in several other nineteenth-century men whose early lives were dominated by their fathers. Anthoney (1975) presents several cases of such self-therapy, while Erikson (1968) discusses William James's struggle to break free from the depressing legacy of his father's early rule. George and George's analysis of Woodrow Wilson (1956) shows still another version of the connection of adult struggles with father figures to the early father-son relationship, though Wilson never worked his conflicts through in any sense. Most striking, perhaps, is the case of John Stuart Mill (see Mazlish, 1974), whose early education was dominated by a father who, if he was not as intrusive and sadistic as Doctor Schreber, was certainly as omnipresent and forceful. Mill underwent a psychological crisis analogous to Schreber's, though by no means as severe, from which he emerged with a new philosophy that championed women's rights and the autonomy of the individual. When, in his essay, 'On Liberty,' Mill says

> Spontaneity forms no part of the ideal of the majority of moral and social reformers, but is rather looked on with jealousy, as a troublesome and perhaps rebellious obstruction to the general acceptance of what these reformers, in their own judgment, think would be best for mankind (Mazlish, p. 147)

he is no doubt speaking from his own early experience with his moral-reformer father, just as Schreber does when he describes God's inability to understand living human beings.

9   Many persons with whom I have discussed my interpretation of Schreber have raised the question of the role of his mother - and one might add his sisters, his wife and other significant women - whose absence is quite striking. In reply, I would say that his mother is nowhere and yet she is everywhere. The fact that Schreber's mother is just mentioned in

passing as a wife who followed the Doctor's dictates in raising her children illustrates the male-dominated quality of this society in which the
significance of mothers, women and the qualities associated with them,
were minimized. Yet these same qualities were everywhere since the one-
sided masculine men were constantly fighting against their own need and
longing for mother love. I hope my analysis has shown that it is a
positively-valued maternal love that finally emerges in Schreber as contrasted, for example, with the hostile attack on mother and the feminine
symbolically expressed in the lives of some male homosexuals. Schreber
must have received enough maternal care to provide the basis for the
identification with these qualities that are eventually integrated into
his postpsychotic personality.

CHAPTER 6 AGGRESSION, DEATH AND THE DISCONTENTS OF CIVILIZATION

1   A detailed critical discussion of aggression and the many theoretical complexities surrounding it is provided by Erich Fromm in his book, 'The
Anatomy of Human Destructiveness' (1973).
2   In her follow-up study of Anna O., Freeman (1972) notes that she
devoted the remainder of her life to aiding young girls who had been
abandoned. Robert Lifton, in an important discussion of the theoretical
neglect of the broad theme of death and the continuity of life in psychoanalytic theory, has this to say about the case:
> Anna O., for example, is properly understood as a mourning reaction.
> The hysteria followed very quickly upon the death of Anna's father and
> had much to do with her reaction to that death. Her conception of
> being alive became altered in such a way that merely to *live* and *feel* -
> to exist as a sexual being - was dangerous, unpermissible, and a
> violation of an unspoken pact with the dead person. Whether or not
> there is a mourning reaction directly involved, hysteria tends to
> involve either this form of statis or its seeming opposite, exaggerated
> movement or activity that serves as a similar barrier against feeling
> and living. These patterns again resemble those I encountered among
> Hiroshima survivors (1974, p. 285).
3   From a letter to Marie Bonapart written in 1937 (Freud, 1960, p. 436).
4   Roy Schafer, in a perceptive discussion of the 'patriarchal perspective'
in Freud's theories, notes:
> These realizations establish, of course, the basis for the mother's
> great authority. Clinical analysts know that this mother's authority
> stays with her children throughout their subsequent lives. For her
> children, the prospect of being abandoned by her physically and
> emotionally, really or in fantasy, never loses its painful, if not
> terrifying aspect. If anxiety over castration at the father's hand
> threatens to undermine the boy's narcissistic integrity and his
> present and future masculine sexuality, anxiety over losing the
> mother or her love threatens to undermine the boy's and girl's very
> sense of worth or right to exist, and for both she is even a castrat-
> ing figure of some consequence as well! (1973, p. 278).
5   See the work of Gregory Bateson and his collaborators (Bateson et al.,
1956; Bateson, 1972) and the evidence presented by Lidz (1963); Laing
and Easterson (1964) and the anthropologist Jules Henry (1971).
6   The connection of women-love-sexuality-death was not just a theoretical
one, as Freud reveals in his dream of the 'Three Fates' (see 'The Interpretation of Dreams,' pp. 204-6). The associations to this dream take
him back to the childhood feelings of hunger, love, man's dependence
on woman and the theme of life and death. He recalls how, as a little
boy, his mother taught him 'we were all made of earth and must therefore return to earth.' His associations then go to the years in Brücke's
laboratory, 'in which I spent the happiest hours of my student life, free
from all other desires - in complete contrast to the desires which were
now plaguing me in my dreams' (p. 206). Thus, he recalls a time when

both sexuality and the awareness of death - both fused in the symbolic image of the earth mother (the 'Three Fates') - were banished to his unconscious as he pursued the goals of science and ambition in the all-male world of scientific research.

This dream, and much else that emerged in the self-analysis, shows Freud moving beyond the narrow man-against-nature position of his earlier scientific and masculine commitments; it reveals him opening up to those repressed themes and feelings within himself associated with feminine qualities and the human connections with nature. (For a related discussion of the emergence of Freud's unconscious feminine side in the self-analysis see Erikson's discussion of -The Dream Specimen of Psycho-analysis- (1954).)

BIBLIOGRAPHY

Abt-Garrison (1965), 'History of Pediatrics,' Saunders, Philadelphia.
Amacher, M.P. (1965), Freud's Neurological Education and its Influence on
    Psychoanalytic Theory, 'Psychological Issues,' 4, no. 4 (monograph no. 16).
Anthoney, J.B. (1975), Self-therapy in Adolescence, 'Adolescent Psychiatry,'
    3, pp. 6-24.
Bakan, D. (1967), 'On Method: Toward a Reconstruction of Psychological
    Investigation,' Jossey-Bass, San Francisco.
Bateson, G. (1972), 'Steps to an Ecology of Mind,' Ballantine Books, New
    York.
——, Jackson, D.D., Haley, J., and Weakland, J. (1956), Toward a Theory
    of Schizophrenia, 'Behavioural Science,' 1, pp. 253-4.
Blum, H. (1974), The Borderline Childhood of the Wolfman, 'Journal of the
    American Psychoanalytic Association,' 22, pp. 721-42.
Bowlby, J. (1969), 'Attachment and Loss,' vol. 1: 'Attachment,' Basic Books,
    New York.
—— (1973), 'Attachment and Loss,' vol. 2: 'Separation,' Basic Books, New
    York.
Breger, L. (1967), Function of Dreams, 'Journal of Abnormal Psychology
    Monograph,' 72, no. 5, pp. 1-28.
——,(ed.)(1969), 'Clinical-Cognitive Psychology: Models and Integrations,'
    Prentice-Hall, Englewood Cliffs.
Chein, I. (1972), 'The Science of Behavior and the Image of Man,' Basic
    Books, New York.
Colby, K.M. (1955), 'Energy and Structure in Psychoanalytic Theory,' Ronald
    Press, New York.
De Mause, L. (1974a), The Evolution of Childhood, in 'The History of Child-
    hood,' ed. L. De Mause.
—— (1974b), 'The History of Childhood,' Psychohistory Press, New York.
Despert, J.L. (1965), 'The Emotionally Disturbed Child: Then and Now,'
    Brunner, New York.
Deutsch, F. (1957), A Footnote to Freud's Fragment of an Analysis of a Case
    of Hysteria, 'Psychoanalytic Quarterly,' 26, pp. 159-67.
DeVore, I. and Konner, M.J. (1974), Infancy in Hunter Gatherer Life: an
    ethological perspective, in 'Ethology and Psychiatry,' ed. N.F. White,
    University of Toronto Press.
Erikson, E. (1950), 'Childhood and Society,' Norton, New York.
—— (1954), The Dream Specimen of Psychoanalysis, 'Journal of the American
    Psychoanalytic Association,' 2, pp. 5-56.
—— (1964), Psychological Reality and Historical Actuality, in 'Insight and
    Responsibility,' Norton, New York, pp. 159-215.
—— (1968), 'Identity: Youth and Crisis,' Norton, New York.
Esman, A.H. (1973), The Primal Scene: a review and a reconsideration,
    'Psychoanalytic Study of the Child,' 28, pp. 49-82.
Fingarette, H. (1963), 'The Self in Transformation: Psychoanalysis, Philosophy
    and the Life of the Spirit,' Basic Books, New York.
Freeman, L. (1972), 'The Story of Anna O.,' Walker, New York.
Freud, S. (1954), 'The Origins of Psychoanalysis: Letters to Wilhelm Fliess
    (1887-1902),' Basic Books, New York.
—— (1895), 'The Project for a Scientific Psychology,' Standard Edition, vol.
    1, pp. 295-397, Hogarth Press, London, 1966.
—— (1895), 'The Studies on Hysteria,' Standard Edition, vol. 2, Hogarth
    Press, London, 1955.

Freud, S. (1898), 'Sexuality in the Aetiology of the Neuroses,' Standard
    Edition, vol. 3, pp. 261-86, Hogarth Press, London, 1962.
—— (1900), 'the Interpretation of Dreams,' Standard Edition, vols. 4 and 5,
    Hogarth Press, London, 1953.
—— (1901), 'The Psychopathology of Everyday Life,' Standard Edition, vol.
    6, Hogarth Press, London, 1960.
—— (1905a), 'Fragment of an Analysis of a Case of Hysteria,' Standard
    Edition, vol. 7, pp. 3-122, Hogarth Press, London, 1953.
—— (1905b), 'Three Essays on the Theory of Sexuality,' Standard Edition,
    vol. 7, pp. 125-245, Hogarth Press, London, 1953.
—— (1905c), 'Jokes and Their Relation to the Unconscious,' Standard Edition,
    vol. 8, Hogarth Press London, 1960.
—— (1909), Notes upon a Case of Obsessional Neurosis,' Standard
    Edition, vol. 10, pp. 153-318, Hogarth Press, London, 1955.
—— (1911), 'Psychoanalytic Notes on an Autobiographical Account of a Case
    of Paranoia (dementia paranoides),' Standard Edition, vol. 12, pp. 3-82,
    Hogarth Press, London, 1958.
—— (1913), 'Totem and Taboo,' Standard Edition, vol. 13, pp. 1-161, Hogarth
    Press, London, 1953.
—— (1914), 'On Narcissism: An Introduction,' Standard Edition, vol. 14, pp.
    67-102, Hogarth Press, London, 1957.
—— (1915a), 'Instincts and their Vicissitudes,' Standard Edition, vol. 14, pp.
    109-40, Hogarth Press, London, 1957.
—— (1915b), 'Observations on Transference Love (further recommendations
    on the technique of psychoanalysis III),' Standard Edition, vol. 12, pp.
    157-71, Hogarth Press, London, 1958.
—— (1917), 'Mourning and Melancholia,' Standard Edition, vol. 14, pp. 237-58,
    Hogarth Press, London, 1957.
—— (1918), 'From the History of an Infantile Neurosis,' Standard Edition,
    vol. 17, pp. 1-122, Hogarth Press, London, 1955.
—— (1920a),'Beyond the Pleasure Principle,' Standard Edition, vol. 18,
    pp. 1-64, Hogarth Press, London, 1955.
—— (1920b), 'The Psychogenesis of a Case of Homosexuality in a Woman,'
    Standard Edition, vol. 18, pp. 145-76, Hogarth Press, London, 1955.
—— (1923), 'The Ego and the Id,' Standard Edition, vol. 19, pp. 1-66,
    Hogarth Press, London, 1961.
—— (1925), 'An Autobiographical Study,' Standard Edition, vol. 20, pp. 1-74,
    Hogarth Press, London, 1959.
—— (1926), 'Inhibitions, Symptoms and Anxiety,' Standard Edition, vol. 20,
    pp. 75-174, Hogarth Press, London, 1959.
—— (1927), 'the Future of an Illusion,' Standard Edition, vol. 21, pp. 1-56,
    Hogarth Press, London, 1961.
—— (1930), 'Civilization and its Discontents,' Standard Edition, vol. 21, pp.
    57-145, Hogarth Press, London, 1961.
—— (1931), 'Female Sexuality,' Standard Edition, vol. 21, pp. 221-43,
    Hogarth Press, London, 1961.
—— (1933), 'The New Introductory Lectures on Psychoanalysis,' Standard
    Edition, vol. 22, pp. 1-182, Hogarth Press, London, 1964.
—— (1960), 'The Letters of Sigmund Freud,' ed. E. Freud, Basic Books,
    New York.
Fromm, E. (1973), 'The Anatomy of Human Destructiveness,' Holt, Rinehart,
    & Winston, New York.
Gardiner, M. (ed.) (1971), 'The Wolfman,' Basic Books, New York.
George, A.L. and George, J.L. (1956), 'Woodrow Wilson and Colonel House:
    A Personality Study,' John Day, New York.
Gill, M.M. and Holtzman, P.S. (1976), Psychology versus Metapsychology:
    Psychoanalytic Essays in Memory of George S. Klein, 'Psychological Issues,'
    9, no. 4 (monograph no. 36).
Henry, J. (1971), 'Pathways to Madness,' Random House, New York.
Holt, R.R. (1965), A Review of Some of Freud's Biological Assumptions
    and Their Influence on His Theories, in 'Psychoanalysis and Current

Biological Thought,' ed. N.S. Greenfield and W.C. Lewis, University of
Wisconsin Press, Madison. pp. 93-124.
Holt, R.R. (1967), The Development of Primary Process, a structural view,
in 'Motives and Thought: Psychoanalvtic Essays in Memory of David
Rapaport,' ed. R.R. Holt, 'Psychological Issues,' 5, nos 2-3 (monograph
nos 18-19), pp. 345-83.
—— (1976), Drive and Wish? A reconsideration of the psychoanalytic theory
of motivation, in 'Psychology versus Metapsychology: Psychoanalytic
Essays in Memory of George S. Klein,' ed. M.M. Gill and P.S. Holzman,
'Psychological Issues,' 9, no. 4 (monograph no. 36), pp. 158-97.
Hunt, D. (1970), 'Parents and Children in History,' Basic Books, New York.
Jones, E. (1953-7), 'The Life and Work of Sigmund Freud,' 3 vols, Basic
Books, New York.
Jones, N.B. and Konner, M.J. (1976), !Kung Knowledge of Animal Behavior,
in 'Kalahari Hunter-Gatherers,' ed. R.B. Lee and I. DeVore, Harvard
University Press, Cambridge, Mass.
Jones, W.T. (1972), World Views: their nature and function, 'Contemporary
Anthropology,' 13, pp. 79-109.
—— (1977), What's the Use of the Humanities?, 'Engineering and Science,'
January-February, pp. 4-8.
Kitay, P.H. (1963), Symposium on the Schreber Case, 'International Journal
of Psychoanalysis,' 44, pp. 191-227.
Klein, G.S. (1976), 'Psychoanalytic Theory: An Exploration of Essentials,'
International Universities Press, New York.
Koch, S. (1959), Epilogue, in 'Psychology: A Study of a Science,' vol. 3,
ed. S. Koch, McGraw-Hill, New York, pp. 729-88.
Kohut, H. (1977), 'The Restoration of the Self,' International Universities
Press, New York.
Konner, M.J. (1972), Aspects of the Developmental Ethology of a Foraging
People, in 'Ethological Studies of Child Behaviour,' ed. N.B. Jones,
Cambridge University Press, pp. 285-304.
Kuhn, T.S. (1962), 'The Structure of Scientific Revolutions,' University
of Chicago Press.
Laing, R.D. (1960), 'The Divided Self,' Penguin, Baltimore.
—— (1967), 'The Politics of Experience,' Pantheon Books, New York.
—— (1969), 'The Politics of the Family,' Pantheon Books, New York.
Laing, R.D. and Esterson, A. (1964), 'Sanity, Madness and the Family,'
Tavistock Publications, London.
Laplanche, J. (1976), 'Life and Death in Psychoanalysis,' Johns Hopkins
University Press, Baltimore.
Lee, R.B. and DeVore, I. (eds) (1968), 'Man the Hunter,' Aldine-Atherton,
Chicago.
—— (1976), 'Kalahari Hunter-Gatherers,' Harvard University Press, Cambridge.
Leites, N. (1971), 'The New Ego,' Science House, New York.
Lewin, K.K. (1973), Dora Revisited, 'Psychoanalytic Review', 60, pp. 519-32.
Lidz, T. (1963), 'The Family and Human Adaptation,' International Univers-
ities Press, New York.
Lifton, R.J. (1974), The Sense of Immortality: on death and the continuity
of life, in 'Explorations in Psychohistory: The Wellfleet Papers,' ed. R.J.
Lifton and E. Olson, Simon & Schuster, New York, pp. 271-87.
—— (1976), 'The Life of the Self,' Simon & Schuster, New York.
Loevinger, J. (1966), Three Principles for a Psychoanalytic Psychology,
'Journal of Abnormal Psychology,' 71, pp. 432-43.
—— (1976), 'Ego Development,' Jossey-Bass, San Francisco.
Maccoby, E.E. and Jacklin, C.N. (1974), 'The Psychology of Sex Differences,'
Stanford University Press.
Marcus, S. (1974), Freud and Dora: story, history, case history, 'Partisan
Review,' 41, pp. 12-23 and 89-108.
Marshall, L. (1976), 'The !Kung of Nyae Nyae,' Harvard University Press,
Cambridge, Mass.
Marvick, E.W. (1974), Nature versus Nurture: patterns and trends in

seventeenth-century French childrearing, in 'The History of Childhood,' ed. L. DeMause, Psychohistory Press, New York, pp. 259-301.

Mazlish, B. (1974), The Mills: father and son, in 'Explorations in Psychohistory: the Wellfleet Papers,' ed. R.J. Lifton and E. Olson, Simon & Schuster, New York, pp. 136-48.

Miller, J.B. (ed.) (1973), 'Psychoanalysis and Women,' Penguin, Harmondsworth.

—— (1976), 'Toward a New Psychology of Women,' Beacon Press, Boston.

Mitchell, J. (1974), 'Psychoanalysis and Feminism,' Pantheon Books, New York.

Niederland, W.G. (1963), Further Data and Memorabilia Pertaining to the Schreber Case, 'International Journal of Psychoanalysis,' 44, pp. 201-7.

—— (1974), 'The Schreber Case: Profile of a Paranoid Personality,' Quadrangle, New York.

Peck, E.C. (1979), The Wolfman's Mothers, thesis, Southern California Psychoanalytic Institute.

Peterfreund, E. (1971), Information, Systems and Psychoanalysis, 'Psychological Issues,' no. 2-3 (monograph nos 25-6).

Piaget, J. (1952), 'Play, Dreams and Imitation in Childhood,' Norton, New York, 1962.

Polanyi, M. (1958), 'Personal Knowledge,' University of Chicago Press.

—— (1966), 'The Tacit Dimension,' Doubleday, New York.

Pribram, K.H. and Gill, M.M. (1976), 'Freud's 'Project' Reassessed,' Basic Books, New York.

Rapaport, D. (1959), The Structure of Psychoanalytic Theory: a systematizing attempt, in 'Psychology: A Study of a Science,' vol. 3, ed. S. Koch, McGraw-Hill, New York, pp. 55-183.

—— and Gill, M.M. (1959), The Points of View and Assumptions of Metapsychology, 'International Journal of Psychoanalysis,' 40, pp. 153-62.

Ricoeur, P. (1970), 'Freud and Philosophy: An Essay on Interpretation,' Yale University Press, New Haven.

Rosenblatt, A.D. and Thickstun, J.T. (1977), Modern Psychoanalytic Concepts in a General Psychology, 'Psychological Issues,' nos 2-3 (monograph nos 42-3).

Rubinstein, B.B. (1967), Explanation and Mere Description: a meta-scientific examination of certain aspects of the psychoanalytic theory of motivation, in 'Motives and Thought: Psychoanalytic Essays in Memory of David Rapaport,' ed. R.R. Holt, 'Psychological Issues,' 5, nos 2-3 (monograph nos 18-19), pp. 18-77.

Rycroft, C. (1967), 'Psychoanalysis Observed,' Coward-McCann, New York.

Schafer, R. (1968), 'Aspects of Internalization,' International Universities Press, New York.

—— (1973), The Idea of Resistance, 'International Journal of Psychoanalysis,' 54, pp. 259-85.

—— (1976), 'A New Language for Psychoanalysis,' Yale University Press, New Haven.

Schatzman, M. (1973), 'Soul Murder: Persecution in the Family,' Random House, New York.

Schreber, D.P. (1903), 'Denkwürdigkeiten eines Nervenkranken,' Oswald, Mutze, Leipzig. Trans. and ed. I. Macalpine and R.A. Hunter, 'Memoirs of My Nervous Illness,' Dawson, London, 1955.

Shakow, D. and Rapaport, D. (1964), The Influence of Freud on American Psychology, 'Psychological Issues,' 4, no. 1 (monograph no. 13).

Skura, M. (1981), 'The Critic and the Psychoanalyst: Literary Uses of the Psychoanalytic Process,' Yale University Press, New Haven.

Stoller, R.J. (1968), 'Sex and Gender,' vol. 1, Science House, New York.

—— (1972), The 'Bedrock' of Masculinity and Feminity: Bisexuality, 'Archives of General Psychiatry,' 26, pp. 207-12.

—— (1975), 'Perversion: The Erotic Form of Hatred,' Pantheon Books, New York.

—— (1979), 'Sexual Excitement: Dynamics of Erotic Life,' Pantheon Books,

New York.
Stone, L. (1974), The Massacre of Innocements, 'New York Review of Books'.
Strachey, J. (1966), Editor's introduction to project for a scientific psychology, in Standard Edition, S. Freud, vol. 1 (1886-99): 'Prepsychoanalytic Publications and Unpublished Drafts,' Hogarth Press, London, pp. 283-93.
Taylor, G.R. (1954), 'Sex in History,' Vanguard Press, New York.
—— (1958), 'The Angel-Makers: A Study in the Psychological Origins of Historical Change, 1750-1850,' Heinemann, London.
Turnbull, C. (1961), 'The Forest People,' Simon & Schuster, New York.
—— (1965), 'Wayward Servants,' Natural History Press, New York.
Whorf, B.L. (1956), 'Language, Thought and Reality,' MIT Press, Cambridge, Mass.
Wilden, A. (1968), 'The Language of the Self: The Function of Language in Psychoanalysis by Jacques Lacan,' Johns Hopkins University Press, Baltimore.
Wishy, B. (1968), 'The Child and the Republic: The Dawn of Modern American Child Nurture,' University of Pennsylvania Press, Philadelphia.
Yankelovich, D. and Barrett, W. (1970), 'Ego and Instinct,' Random House, New York.

INDEX